Predicting Internalizing Problems in At-Risk Children and Adolescents

Tawnyea L. Bolme-Lake

DISSERTATION.COM

Boca Raton

Predicting Internalizing Problems in At-Risk Children and Adolescents

Dissertation.com
Boca Raton, Florida
USA • 2008

ISBN-10: 1-59942-659-5
ISBN-13: 978-1-59942-659-4

PREDICTING INTERNALIZING PROBLEMS IN

AT-RISK CHILDREN AND ADOLESCENTS

By

Tawnyea L. Bolme-Lake

A Dissertation Presented in Partial Fulfillment

of the Requirements for the Degree

Doctor of Philosophy

Capella University

August 2007

PREDICTING INTERNALIZING PROBLEMS IN

AT-RISK CHILDREN AND ADOLESCENTS

by

Tawnyea L. Bolme-Lake

has been approved

August 2007

WILLIAM CAMERON, Ph.D., Faculty Mentor and Chair

KELLEY CHAPPELL, Ph.D., Committee Member

ANTANAS LEVINSKAS, Ph.D., Committee Member

GARVEY HOUSE, Ph.D. Dean, School of Psychology

A Dissertation Presented in Partial Fulfillment

Of the Requirements for the Degree

Doctor of Philosophy

Capella University

August 2007

Abstract

Internalizing problems are common among adolescents. Poor outcomes such as academic failure, substance misuse, and adult mental health problems have all been linked to internalizing problems. Although the potential effects are serious, internalizing disorders tend to be under-diagnosed and under-treated. To compound the problem, research in the area of internalizing disorders continues to lag behind that of other disorders. In the last ten years, however, research has indicated that relationships with parents, gender, and self-esteem are factors associated with internalizing disorders. To clarify the relationships between these factors, archival data was collected from an electronic database in a school district in northeastern Minnesota. This database includes the results of the Behavior Assessment System for Children-2; Self-Report of Personality (BASC-2) of children and adolescents who have taken it as a part of a special education evaluation. The BASC-2 is a norm-referenced questionnaire that measures emotions and self-perceptions. Factorial analysis of variance was used determine whether the degree of internalizing problems differ between relationships with parents, gender, and self-esteem groups, reflected by scores on the Parent Relations, Self-Esteem, and Internalizing Problems scales included in the BASC-2. Further, multiple regression procedures were used to determine if the combination of the quality of relations with parents, gender, and level of self-esteem predicts the degree of internalizing problems experienced by at-risk children and adolescents. Contrary to past studies, results did not show gender significant differences in the degree of internalizing problems reported. Results did, however, indicate that the degree of reported internalizing problems was related to the quality of parent relationships and self-esteem. Specifically, children and adolescents who reported poor relationships with their parents reported a significantly greater degree of internalizing problems than those who reported average or better relationships with their parents. Likewise, children and adolescents who reported low self-esteem reported a significantly greater degree of internalizing problems than those with average or better self-esteem. In addition, gender, the quality of parent relations, and level of self-esteem showed a predictive relationship with internalizing problems. The implications of these findings, as well as directions for future research were discussed.

Acknowledgments

There are many individuals to who I wish to acknowledge for making this project possible. Faculty from Capella University, professionals from the public school district from which the data was gathered, as well as my friends and family all played an important role in the success of this project. Without their support, completion would not have been possible.

First, I would like to extend my sincere gratitude to the members of my dissertation committee. Dr. William Cameron, mentor and dissertation chair, provided support, guidance, and expertise. Dr. Antanas Levinskas and Dr. Kelley Chappell also provided a good deal of support and encouragement throughout this process.

Second, I would like to thank several top-notch professionals from the public school district from which the data was gathered. Specifically, Dr. Keith Dixon and Marci Hoff granted me permission to use data from their school district, and Angela Sepp and Cody Chamberlain assisted in the electronic data collection.

Third, I would like to thank the "Kids Table". Their support made my educational goals seem attainable; their intellect challenged me and made me proud to be a part of such an accomplished group.

Fourth, I would like to thank my nearest and dearest friends for sticking with me throughout this journey. My "sisters", Margie and Lisa, my "couple friends", Dave and Shelley, Will and Sue, Chuck and Vicky... all kept me laughing, smiling, and having fun throughout the process.

And finally, I would like to give a heartfelt thanks to my family. My husband Ron has provided unconditional love and unwavering support throughout all of my educational endeavors. His belief in me gave me the strength to see this to completion.

My amazing children Kaitlyn and Alek provided daily inspiration. When difficulties were

encountered, their smiling faces and sincere acts of love kept everything in perspective.

Brother D and sister-in-law MP, Baby Bolme, Bob, Char, Rob, Karie and the kids… each

provided helpful support in one way or another. My parents, Rich and Donna provided

me with the on-going belief that anything is possible. The often-repeated phrase "you can

do anything you put your mind to" resonates in me and has guided me throughout my

life. Thank you!

Table of Contents

List of Tables

List of Figures

CHAPTER 1. INTRODUCTION

Introduction to the Problem

Mental health conditions can be divided into two broad categories, internalizing disorders and externalizing disorders. This approach to classification is based on the empirical work of Achenbach and colleagues (Achenbach, 1966, 1985; Achenbach & Edelbrock, 1978; Achenbach & McConaughy, 1996). Using multivariate factor analysis, two large groups of conditions were identified. Inner-directed, over-controlled behaviors that cause emotional distress in the self were classified as internalizing disorders. In contrast, behavior disorders that create conflicts within the environment or with others were categorized as externalizing disorders (Reynolds, 1990).

Internalizing disorders such as anxiety and depression are common among children and adolescents. In fact, the estimated prevalence of anxiety disorders in children and adolescents is 13% (U.S. Surgeon General, 1999). In addition, some studies suggest that as many as 20% of adolescents will experience at least one episode of clinically significant depression in their lifetimes (Birmaher et al., 1996; Garber, 2000; Lewinsohn & Essau, 2002). Both of these disorders are included within the cluster of internalizing disorders (Achenbach, 1966, 1985; Achenbach & Edelbrock, 1978; Achenbach & McConaughy, 1996).

Although researchers cite high prevalence rates for these disorders, some argue that statistics actually underestimate their true incidence (Reynolds, 1990). This occurs because these disorders present symptoms that are not always observable (Laurent &

1

Landau, 1993). In addition, the inner-directed nature of these disorders does not affect others as the outer-directed externalizing disorders tend to, nor do they present behavior management challenges for parents, teachers, or mental health professionals. As a result, internalizing disorders are often overlooked (Reynolds, 1992).

Even when internalizing disorders are diagnosed, research suggests that they are often under-treated. Wu et al. (1999) found that youngsters with externalizing problems are likely to receive services through mental health organizations and schools. In contrast, youngsters with internalizing disorders, such as depression, are more likely to receive services solely in their schools. In other words, children and adolescents with internalizing-type disorders may get less treatment than those with other types of disorders. This discrepancy occurs because externalizing disorders tend to cause more distress in others, causing parents to seek additional support from community agencies (1999).

Untreated internalizing disorders are related to serious problems. Academic failure is one of the problems associated with internalizing disorders (National Association of School Psychologists, 2002; Rapport, Denney, Chung, & Hustace, 2001; Reynolds, 1992). Rapport et al. (2001) conducted a study using a sample of 325 children and adolescents ages 5 - 7. Measures such as intelligence, classroom performance, internalizing behavior, short-term memory, and vigilance were used to examine the relationship between internalizing problems and classroom performance. Results indicated that internalizing behavior, defined in this study as anxiety, depression, and withdrawal, contributed significantly to the prediction of classroom performance "over and above the effects of intelligence" and all other factors (p. 548).

2

Substance misuse is another problem related to internalizing disorders (Kubik, Lytle, Birnbaum, Murray, & Perry, 2003; Lillehoj, Trudeau, Spoth, & Wickrama, 2004; Loeber, Stouthamer-Loeber, & White, 1999; Wang, Fitzhugh, & Westerfield, 1994). Kubik et al. (2003) surveyed 3,621 12 and 13 year-olds in 16 different middle schools in Minnesota. Information was collected for gender, age, race/ethnicity, depressive symptoms, smoking, alcohol use, and use of marijuana and inhalants. Results showed that in both boys and girls, depressive symptoms were strongly associated with monthly alcohol and inhalant use. Monthly smoking and heavy drinking were associated with depressive symptoms in girls only. This suggests that the association between substance use and internalizing disorders is a concern in young adolescents as well as older adolescents. It also underscores the existence of gender differences.

Internalizing disorders in childhood and adolescence are also associated with mental health problems later in adulthood (Pine, Cohen, Cohen, & Brook, 1999; National Association of School Psychologists, 2003). Pine et al. analyzed a sample of 776 adolescents with depressive symptoms who had psychiatric evaluations completed in 1983, 1985, and 1992. Results showed that adolescent depressive symptoms strongly predicted adult major depression. In fact, adolescents with clinical depression were 2 - 3 times more likely to have at least one major depressive episode as an adult.

Despite the high prevalence of these disorders and the associated detrimental effects, research in the area of internalizing disorders lags behind in comparison to research in the area of externalizing disorders (Compton, Burns, Egger, & Robertson, 2002). This lag is especially evident with respect to the child and adolescent population.

Background of the Study

The 1970s marked the beginning of research on internalizing disorders. During this time, research efforts focused on the nature and treatment of these disorders in adults (Reynolds, 1992). However, it wasn't until the 1980s that the study of internalizing disorders trickled down to the child and adolescent population. Prior to that, children and adolescents with internalizing symptoms were viewed as going through normal, but difficult, developmental stages in their lives. The common belief was they would simply "grow out" of their symptoms (1992). Reynolds argued that this growing attention to child and adolescent internalizing disorders stemmed in part from a rapidly increasing suicide rate among adolescents in the 1950s, 1960s, and 1970s. The publication of the Diagnostic and Statistical Manual of Mental Disorders-III in 1980 also sparked interest in the phenomenon of internalizing disorders of childhood and adolescence (1992).

Statement of the Problem

Since the 1980s, studies have identified that certain factors, such as gender, put some individuals at a higher risk of developing internalizing disorders. Specifically, many studies indicate that girls are far more likely to develop internalizing disorders than boys (Leadbeater, Blatt, & Quinlan, 1995; Crawford, Cohen, Midlarsky, & Brook, 2001; Kubik, et al., 2003; Jose & Ratcliff, 2004; Ronnlund & Karlsson, 2006). Researchers have also identified certain factors that may make some children and adolescents less vulnerable to internalizing disorders. Quality relationships between adolescents and their parents, as well as high self-esteem have been implicated as protective factors against problems in psychological adjustment (Schweitzer, Seth-Smith, & Callan, 1992; Delaney,

4

1996; Bryne, 2000; Kliewer, Murrelle, & Meja, 2001; Erkolahti, Ilonen, Saarijavi, & Terho, 2003; Marsh, Parada, & Ayotte, 2004; Reid, 2004; Manders, Scholte, Janssens, & De Bruyn, 2006; Margolin, 2006; Ronnlund & Karlsson, 2006).

Although certain risk factors and protective factors have been identified, research has been limited to simple relationships between these variables; no research to date has examined the possible interactions between these factors. In addition, researchers have not explored the potential predictive relationship between this combination of factors and the degree of internalizing problems reported by children and adolescents. This study fills those gaps in the literature.

Purpose of the Study

Given the high prevalence of internalizing disorders, the associated detrimental effects, and the relative lack of research on internalizing disorders in comparison to externalizing disorders, additional research is needed to identify possible factors or combination of factors that put adolescents at a higher risk for developing these disorders. This study examines whether girls experience greater internalizing problems in comparison to boys, and whether the lack of quality relationships with parents and low self-esteem are associated with a high degree of internalizing problems. It will also examine interaction effects. Additionally, it employs multiple regression procedures to determine if any of these factors or combination of factors, have a predictive relationship with internalizing problems.

Significance of the Study

This study identifies the potentially complex interplay between the factors of quality of relations with parents, gender, level of self-esteem, and degree of internalizing problems. It is expected that these findings will be useful in identifying unique interactions between these variables. As a result, a profile of characteristics that put children and adolescents at a higher risk for development of internalizing disorders will be identified. Identification of risk factors may, in turn, help guide interventions for these groups.

Nature of the Study

This study uses a causal-comparative factorial design to examine how the quality of parent relationships, gender, and level of self-esteem are related to internalizing problems in the at-risk population of children and adolescents. Specifically, this study uses archival data to determine whether there are interactions between and among these factors. In addition, this research uses multiple regression procedures to examine whether any of these variables or combination of variables can predict future internalizing problems in at-risk children and adolescents.

Research Questions

1. Is there a statistically significant difference in the degree of internalizing problems between the two Relations with Parents groups (Average/Above Average, At-Risk/Clinically Significant) as measured by the BASC-2?

2. Is there a statistically significant difference in the degree of internalizing problems between the two gender groups (Male, Female) as measured by the BASC-2?

3. Is there a statistically significant difference in the degree of internalizing problems between the two Self-Esteem groups (Average/Above Average, At-Risk/Clinically Significant) as measured by the BASC-2?

4. Does the combination of quality of relations with parents, gender, and level of self-esteem have a predictive relationship with the degree of internalizing problems reported by at-risk children and adolescents?

Definition of Terms

There are several terms related to this study that require further explanation. These terms will be used throughout the remainder of the study as defined in this section.

At-Risk Children and Adolescents

For the purpose of this research, at-risk children and adolescents will refer to youngsters between the ages of 8-18 that either receive special education services as a result of an identified emotional/behavioral disorder or have been referred for a special education evaluation because an emotional/behavioral disorder is suspected. This population is the focus of this study.

At-Risk/Clinically Significant Relations with Parents

According to Reynolds and Kamphaus (2004), T-scores of 31 - 40 on any adaptive measure, such as Parent Relations, are considered At-Risk. Scores that fall within the At-Risk range indicate "the presence of significant problems" or "may signify potential or developing problems that need to be monitored carefully" (p. 16). Likewise, T-scores of 30 and below are considered Clinically Significant in the area of Relations with Parents and "denote a high level of maladaptive behavior" (p. 16). The At-Risk/Clinically Significant Parent Relations group will consist of children and adolescents who reported problems within the parent-child relationship.

At-Risk/Clinically Significant Self-Esteem

In the area of Self-Esteem, T-scores of 31 - 40 are considered At-Risk on the BASC-2 (Reynolds & Kamphaus, 2004). According to Reynolds and Kamphaus, any adaptive measure, including Self-Esteem, that reflects scores that fall within the At-Risk range indicate "the presence of significant problems" or "may signify potential or developing problems that need to be monitored carefully" (p. 16). Likewise, T-scores 30 and below are considered Clinically Significant. Scores that fall within the Clinically Significant range "denote a high level of maladaptive behavior" (Reynolds & Kamphaus, 2004, p. 16). Therefore, children and adolescents in the At-Risk/Clinically Significant Self-Esteem group represent individuals with low self-esteem.

Average/Above Average Relations with Parents

In the area of Relations with Parents, T-scores of 60 and above are considered High or Very High and indicate very positive relations between the parents and the child or adolescent. T-scores of 41 - 59 are considered Average and reflect average quality relationships between the child or adolescent and his or her parents (Reynolds & Kamphaus, 2004). Thus, the Average/Above Average Parent Relations group consists of youngsters who reported average or better relationships with their parents.

8

Average/Above Average Self-Esteem

In the area of Self-Esteem, T-scores of 60 and above are considered High and Very High on the BASC-2 and reflect a level of self-esteem that is better than average. Likewise, T-scores of 41 - 59 are considered Average, and reflect an average level of self-esteem (Reynolds & Kamphaus, 2004). Thus, children and adolescents with Average/Above Average Self-Esteem reflect individuals with average or better self-esteem.

Behavior Assessment System for Children; Second Edition (BASC-2)

The BASC-2 is a multi-method, multidimensional assessment tool that evaluates behavior and self-perceptions of children and adolescents (Reynolds & Kamphaus, 2004). This is one of the evaluation tools used in the school district under study when considering the special education eligibility. It is also the tool that was used to measure the quality of relationships with parents, level of self-esteem, as well as the degree of internalizing problems in this study.

Emotional/Behavioral Disorder (EBD)

According to National Association of School Psychologists (2002), EBD refers to "a condition in which behavioral or emotional responses of an individual in school are so different from his/her generally accepted, age-appropriate, ethnic or cultural norms that they adversely affect performance in such areas as self care, social relationships, personal adjustment, academic progress, classroom behavior, or work adjustment" (para. 3). All of the students whose BASC-2 results were used for this study have been evaluated and identified as having an EBD, another disability, or were suspected of having an EBD.

Internalizing Problems

Internalizing disorders are a group of disorders that are described as inner-directed and over-controlled (Reynolds, 1992). The Internalizing Problems composite score on the BASC-2 Self-Report of Personality includes the scales of Atypicality (tendency to behave in a manner considered odd or strange), Locus of Control, Social Stress, Anxiety, Depression, and Sense of Inadequacy. Reynolds and Kamphaus (2004) consider the Internalizing Problems composite on the BASC-2 as a "broad index of inwardly directed distress."

Parent Relationships

In this study, the quality of the relationship between the child or adolescent and the parents was measured using the Relations with Parents scale on the BASC-2. According to Reynolds and Kamphaus (2004), this scale "surveys the individual's perception of being important in the family, the status of the child-parent relationship, and the child's perception of the degree of parental trust and concern" (p. 78).

Self-Esteem

The level of self-esteem was measured in this study using the Self-Esteem scale on the BASC-2. This scale evaluates the adolescent's satisfaction with one's self, physically and globally (Reynolds & Kamphaus, 2004).

Assumptions and Limitations

There are several key assumptions embedded within this study that are worth noting. The first group of assumptions is related to the quantitative philosophy of this study. With regard to ontology, this research assumes a single reality rather than multiple

10

realities. The epistemology assumes that the researcher and the data are independent entities. The axiology of this study assumes that the researcher's values will not impact the final results. It is also assumed that at least some degree of generalizations will be possible as a result of the study and that causes and effects exist in a linear manner. Finally, this study assumes a deductive method of logic.

The second group of assumptions is related to the use of the BASC-2 as the tool of measurement used in this study. First, it is assumed that the school professionals that administered the BASC-2 as a part of the special education evaluation process followed proper testing and scoring procedures. Second, it is assumed that the students that completed the BASC-2 answered the questions openly and honestly. Third, it is assumed that the demographics of the students that took that BASC-2 in the school district under study roughly match the demographics of the students included in the BASC-2 norm group.

The limitations of this study should also be taken into account when making generalizations from the final results. The first group of limitations is related to the concept of internalizing disorders. Although the distinction between internalizing disorders and externalizing disorders has empirical support (Achenbach, 1966; 1985), it is important to note that not every mental health condition falls neatly into these two categories. Rather, internalizing disorders often have symptoms that overlap with other externalizing disorders (McConaughy & Skiba, 1993). Second, internalizing disorders and externalizing disorders are often co-morbid (1993). Finally, not all researchers agree which specific mental health conditions fall within the category or internalizing disorders (Reynolds, 1992). All of these factors affects the interpretation of the final results.

The second group of limitations involves the generalizability of the results of this study. First, the data comes from a school district in northeastern Minnesota that may not be representative of all at-risk children and adolescents in the United States. Second, the documents used in this study come from a database of students that were either referred for special education evaluation or were already receiving special education services. At-risk students with internalizing problems who have not been evaluated or reevaluated for special education eligibility were not included in this study. Third, this study focused solely on children and adolescents between the ages of 8 and 18. Finally, multicollinearity may exist between the predictor variables. Multicollinearity refers to a situation in which the predictor variables are highly correlated (Howell, 2004). Based on the existing literature, it is possible that gender and self-esteem will be related (Kling, Hyde, Showers, & Buswell, 1999; Quatman & Watson, 2001). Each of these factors limits the generalizability of this study beyond its stated parameters.

Organization of the Remainder of the Study

This study is comprised of five chapters. The first chapter provides an introduction to the problem, background of the of the study, statement of the problem, purpose of the study, research questions, nature of the study, significance of the study, definition of terms, as well as assumptions and limitations. The second chapter thoroughly reviews the literature that is relevant to this study and describes the rationale behind the chosen methodology, design, and measures. The third chapter consists of a description of the research design, target population, section of documents, variables, measures, and procedures, as well as data collection and analysis plans. In addition, expected findings are discussed. Chapter four includes a description of the collected data, verification of assumptions, and the results of the data analyses. Chapter five begins by framing the chapter and reviewing the preliminary results. This is followed by a discussion and interpretation of the results. In addition, strengths and limitations of the study and recommended directions for future research are included. The final section of the chapter ends with a summary and conclusion of the study.

CHAPTER 2. LITERATURE REVIEW

Introduction to the Literature Review

This chapter consists of three main sections. The first section provides a critical review of the research to date that has examined the variables used in this study. The next section describes the rationale for using the chosen methods, design, and measures of this study. The final section concludes the chapter by summarizing the important points discussed within the literature review.

Critical Review of the Relevant Literature

This review examines research specific to the broad category of internalizing disorders when possible. However, research in this area is relatively limited in comparison to research that examines internalizing disorders separately. Thus, this review includes key studies that examine the variables in this study and their relationships to specific disorders that typically fall within the broad category of internalizing disorders.

Gender and Internalizing Problems

Over the years, gender differences in the prevalence internalizing disorders have been well-established. In a meta-analysis, Leadbeater et al. (1995) reviewed more than 20 cross-sectional studies that that examined gender differences in depressive symptoms in adolescents. Depressive symptoms were measured by a variety of self-report questionnaires. The review revealed that 13.5% - 34% of the adolescents in the studies reported at least moderate symptoms, and 5% - 8.6% of the adolescents reported severe depressive symptoms. Prior to puberty, prevalence appeared consistent across genders.

14

However, shortly after puberty, significant gender differences emerged. Some studies reviewed in the meta-analysis reported depressed mood in 56% of girls compared to 36% of boys.

Kubik et al. (2003) conducted a study that examined gender differences in depressive symptoms in a sample of 3621 ethnically diverse 12 - 13 year olds attending school in Minnesota. Depressive symptoms were evaluated using The Center for Epidemiologic Studies Depression Scale (CES-D; Radloff, 1977); gender was obtained from official school records. Thirty-five percent of the total sample reported elevated depressive symptomology. Significantly more girls obtained high scores on the CES-D than boys. Specifically, 40% of the girls reported elevated depressive symptomology compared to 35% of the boys in the study.

Another large study found similar results over a much broader age range than the Kubik et al. study. Jose and Ratcliff (2004) surveyed 2505 adolescents from New Zealand ranging in age from 10 - 20 years. Measures included the Children's Depression Inventory (CDI; Kovacs, 1985), a shortened version of the Children's Manifest Anxiety Scale (CMA; Reynolds & Richmond, 1997), and the Psychosomatic Symptoms Scale (PSS; Andersson, 1981). Results indicated that females reported significantly higher symptoms of depression, anxiety, and psychosomatic complaints than males.

Some studies reported that gender differences are significant only at certain ages. In one such study, Crawford et al. (2001) used a subsample from the Children in the Community Study. The subsample used consisted of 217 adolescents ages that were demographically representative of upstate New York. Internalizing symptoms were measured using the Diagnostic Interview Schedule for Children, Depression and

15

Overanxious Scales (DISC; Costello, Edelbrock, Dulcan, Kalas, & Klaric, 1984) as well as the Depression Scale of the Symptom Checklist-90 (SLC-90; Derogatis, Lipman, Rickles, Uhlenhuth, & Covi, 1974). These measures were administered on four separate occasions, including 1975 (Time 1), 1983 (Time 2), 1985 - 1986 (Time 3), and 1991 - 1993 (Time 4). Significant age-related gender differences emerged. Specifically, females reported significantly higher scores on the DISC and the SCL-90 at ages 16 - 22 (Time 4), but not at ages 9 - 12 (Time 2) or 11 - 15 (Time 3).

Several limitations exist within the literature. Although many studies support the contention that gender differences in internalizing problems exist, conclusions differ depending on the age of the participants. In addition, studies have not focused solely on the at-risk population of children and adolescents, nor have they addressed internalizing problems as a single category. Finally, no studies have investigated the potential interactive effects with gender and other factors such as the quality of parent relationships and the level of self-esteem. This study not only focuses on the at-risk population in the 8 - 18 year-old age range, it examines internalizing problems within the context of a single category. In addition, the relationship between gender and internalizing disorders are also studied within the context of other factors, such as quality of parent-adolescent relations and level of self-esteem. Including these features in the current study extends the current knowledge of gender differences in internalizing disorders.

Self-Esteem and Internalizing Problems

Research on the relationship between self-esteem and the category of internalizing problems is lacking. However, over the years some studies have investigated the relationship between self-esteem and overall mental health and personal adjustment.

16

Others have focused on the relationship between self-esteem and specific disorders that fall within the internalizing problems cluster. Both types of studies were included in this review.

Schweitzer et al. (1992) studied the relationship between self-esteem and psychological adjustment in a group of 66 adolescents ages 12 - 16. Personal adjustment was measured by parent support using the Child Behavior Checklist, which is a 120-item parent report of behavior and social competence (Achenbach & Edelbrock, 1978). Adolescents were divided into two groups, disturbed and non-disturbed, based on their total behavioral problems score on the Child Behavior Checklist. Non-disturbed adolescents, or the control group, were identified based behavioral problems scores that were within normal limits; behavior problems scores that fell outside of the normal limits identified disturbed adolescents. The 102-item Self-Description Questionnaire (SDQ-II; Marsh, 1992) was used to measure self-concept in both groups. Comparisons on general self-concept as well as specific dimensions of self-concept were made between the disturbed and the non-disturbed groups. Results indicated a statistically significant difference between the disturbed and non-disturbed adolescents with respect to global self-esteem, with the non-disturbed group reporting overall higher self-esteem.

Marsh et al. (2004) also examined the relationship between self-esteem and psychological adjustment. Information was collected from 903 multi-ethnic Canadian adolescents in grades 7 and 8. Like the Schweitzer et al. (1992) study, self-concept was measured using the Self-Description Questionnaire II (SDQ-II; Marsh, 1992). Mental health problems were measured using the Achenbach Youth Self-Report (YSR; Achenbach & Edelbrock, 1978). Results revealed a strong positive correlation between self-esteem and emotional stability (.70). In addition, there was a moderate negative correlation between self-esteem and each of the 7 problem factors evaluated by the YSR, including Anxious/Depressed and Somatic Complaints (2004).

In a longitudinal study, Byrne (2000) examined the relationship between anxiety and self-esteem. Three hundred boys and girls aged 12 - 18, were given the Rosenberg Self-Esteem Scale (RSES; Rosenberg, 1965) and the State-Trait Anxiety Inventory (Spielberger, Gorsuch, Lushene, Vagg, & Jacobs, 1983) in grades 7, 9, and 12. The results differed slightly by gender. For the boys, changes in anxiety were directly related to self-esteem in grade 9. In contrast, anxiety varied with self-esteem in grades 7 and 12 for girls. In both genders, anxiety and self-esteem were inversely related.

In a culturally diverse group of 199 college students, Reid (2004) examined various factors that are believed to contribute to well-being, including self-esteem. The Affect Balance Scale (ABS; Bradburn, 1969) was used to evaluate positive affect and negative affect; the Rosenberg Self-Esteem Scale (RSES; Rosenberg, 1965) was used to measure self-esteem. Results indicated that self-esteem was positively correlated to affect balance in the total sample ($r = .62$). For men, self-esteem predicted affect balance ($r = .70$), positive affect ($r = .56$), and negative affect ($r = -.57$). For women, self-esteem predicted affect balance ($r = .56$), positive affect ($r = .36$), and negative affect ($r = -.52$). All results were statistically significant ($p < .001$).

Erkolahti et al. (2003) studied the relationship between self-image and depressive symptoms in a non-clinical sample of 1054 Finnish students in 8th grade. Self-image was evaluated using the Offer Self-Image Questionnaire (OSIQ; Offer, Ostrov, Howard, & Dolan, 1989); depressive symptomology was measured using the Children's Depression

18

Inventory (CDI; Beck, Ward, Mendelson, Mock, & Erbaugh, 1961). Strong correlations were noted between the total score of the OSIQ and the CDI for both genders (girls r = -72; boys r = -.51). In addition, the difference in the strength of the correlations between boys and girls was statistically significant (p < .0001).

The existing literature has demonstrated a relationship between self-esteem and specific internalizing disorders, such as depression and anxiety. Research has also indicated that self-esteem is related to healthy personal adjustment and mental health. However, there were limitations in each of these studies. Schweitzer et al. (1992) used a small sample. In addition, the disturbed adolescents were identified from a clinical-referred sample, which is not likely to be representative beyond that specific population. Erkolahti et al. (2003) used a large sample; however, the sample consisted of students from Finland only. Likewise, Marsh et al. (2004) based their conclusions on a narrow sample of economically disadvantaged French Canadian students; Reid (2004) studied college-age students. Thus, the existing literature has focused on samples that are not representative of the at-risk population that is of interest in this study.

There were additional limitations as well. Byrne (2000) based the conclusions of the study on instruments with out-dated norms. Marsh et al. (2004) used English-language questionnaires that were translated into French prior to administration. It is not known how either of these factors would affect the outcomes of these studies. In addition, no studies have investigated the relationship between self-esteem and the broad category of internalizing problems. Finally, the existing literature has not examined the potential interactive effects between self-esteem and other factors such as gender and the quality of parent-adolescent relationships. The present study adds to the literature by using a

19

comprehensive measurement tool with current norms. It also examines interactions

among variables and predictive relationships. These additions will help fill the gaps in the

existing literature.

Quality of Relationships with Parents and Internalizing Problems

Few studies to date have considered the role that the parent-child plays with the

broad category of internalizing disorders. Researchers have, however, investigated the

relationship between the quality of parent-child relationships and specific disorders that

fall within the internalizing problems cluster. Both types of studies were reviewed to

provide rationale for studying the relationship between the quality of parent-child

relationships and internalizing problems.

Margolin (2006) studied the role that parent support plays with internalizing

problems. This study was conducted with 232 African American youths from 15 6th grade

classrooms near a large midwestern city. Data for internalizing difficulties was collected

using the Depression Self-Rating Scale (DSRS; Birleson, 1981), the Social Anxiety Scale

for Children (La Greca, 1999), and the Loneliness Rating Scale (Asher, Hymel, &

Renshaw, 1984). Social support data was collected using the My Family and Friends

Interview (Reid, Landesman, Treder, & Jaccard, 1989). A significant negative correlation

was noted with regard level of internalizing difficulties and level of family support.

Correlations with family support and activity involvement were: Depression $r = -.49$,

Social Anxiety $r = -.63$, and Loneliness $r = -.93$.

The results of a study conducted by Manders et al. (2006) echoed the results

obtained by Margolin (2006). One hundred-forty Dutch adolescents ranging in age from

11 - 18 years were recruited for this study. Two scales of the Relational Support

Inventory (RSI; Sholte, van Lieshout, & van Aken, 2001) as well as a 9-item version of

the Parent-Adolescent Communication Scale (Gerris et al., 1998) was used to measure

the parent-child relationship. Adolescent problem behavior was evaluated using the

Nijmegen Problem Behavior List, which includes behaviors that fall within either the

externalizing or internalizing cluster (Scholte et al., 2001). Using multiple regression

analysis, higher quality father-adolescent and mother-adolescent relationships predicted a

significantly lower level of internalizing problems.

Longitudinal studies that have examined the quality of parent-child relationships

and the effect on internalizing problems have also reported consistent results. Delaney

(1996) used data from the Penn State Family Relationships Project that included 133

families of 12 - 13 year olds. Parent-adolescent relationships were measured using the

Emotional Autonomy Scale (Steinberg & Silverberg, 1986) and a 4-item subset of the

Parent-Child Intimacy Scale (Blyth, Hill, & Theil, 1982). Confirmatory cluster analysis

procedures were used to identify distinct parent-adolescent relationship types. Three

relationship-types emerged: Individuated, Connected, and Detached. Adolescents with

Individuated relationships reported high levels of closeness with their parents, coupled

with moderate to high levels of autonomy. Adolescents with Connected relationships

were those with even higher levels of closeness with their parents and low levels of

autonomy. Adolescents with Detached relationships reported high autonomy form parents

and low closeness. Depressive symptomology was assessed using the Children's

Depression Inventory (CDI; Kovacs, 1981); anxiety was assessed using the Revised

Children's Anxiety Scale (RCMAS; Reynolds & Richmond, 1979). Data was collected on

two occasions, one year apart. Adolescents who reported Detached relationships with their parents also reported significantly higher symptoms of depression and anxiety than adolescents who reported Connected or Individuated relationships with their parents. Findings were consistent at both times of data collection. No gender differences were noted, with one exception. Girls reported a higher degree of anxiety.

Three primary gaps in the literature were identified with respect to the quality of parent-child relations and its association with internalizing problems. First, the available studies used instruments with relatively old norms to measure the variables. Second, the age and ethnic groups that were examined were not representative of the at-risk population that is the focus of this study. Third, the potential interactions between the quality of parent-child relationships, gender, and self-esteem were not considered. This study uses an instrument with recently updated norms to measure the quality of parent-child relations, self-esteem, and internalizing problems. In addition, the participants consist of a sample of ethnically diverse at-risk children and adolescents. The addition of these factors will broaden the understanding of internalizing problems in at-risk children and adolescents.

Rationale for Methodology, Design, and Measures

This section of the literature review provides the rationale for the chosen approach to this study. The intention of this research is to build upon the existing line of investigations on internalizing disorders in childhood and adolescence. Relationships between gender, quality of parent-child relations, self-esteem, and internalizing problems were investigated; predictive relationships between these variables were explored. Focusing on these areas fills the identified gaps in the existing research on internalizing disorders in at-risk children and adolescents. Methodological, design, and measurement considerations were based on this goal.

Methodology and Design

This study falls under the methodological approach of quantitative research. As such, a deductive approach was used. A deductive approach allows specific predictions to be made from the existing literature (Breakwell & Rose, 2000). The conclusions based on the results of this study will be used to better understand internalizing disorders in at-risk children and adolescents. Specifically, factors and combination of factors that put certain youngsters at risk for internalizing problems are identified and can be used to generalize to children and adolescents with similar at-risk characteristics. Because the intent of this study was to generalize the results to others, quantitative methodology was the most appropriate methodological choice.

Within the methodology of quantitative study, a causal-comparative research design was chosen. Like true experimental designs, causal-comparative designs explore how independent variables affect the dependent variable (Leedy & Ormrod, 2005). However, causal comparative designs differ from true experimental designs in that the independent variable is not manipulated. It would not be possible to assign children and adolescents to the various groups under study (gender, level of self-esteem, quality of parent relations); rather, these variables are pre-existing conditions (2005). Therefore, this study is considered causal-comparative in nature.

Factorial ANOVA is the statistical method that was used to answer the first three research questions. As noted earlier, the first three research questions are:

1. Is there a statistically significant difference in the degree of internalizing problems between the two Relations with Parents groups (Average/Above Average, At-Risk/Clinically Significant) as measured by the BASC-2?

2. Is there a statistically significant difference in the degree of internalizing problems between the two gender groups (Male, Female) as measured by the BASC-2?

3. Is there a statistically significant difference in the degree of internalizing problems between the four Self-Esteem groups (Average/Above Average, At-Risk/Clinically Significant) as measured by the BASC-2?

These research questions seek to determine whether differences between groups exist. Each group has more than one level. Gender has two levels (Male, Female) as does the quality of parent relations as well as the level of self-esteem (Average/Above Average, At-Risk/Clinically Significant). Factorial designs allow comparisons between every level of every factor to every level of every other factor (Howell, 2004). Therefore, a factorial design was the most appropriate design choice to answer the first three research questions.

Howell (2004) describes three primary advantages of using factorial designs. First, factorial designs allow more in-depth interpretation of results and greater generalizability than one-way designs. Second, the interactions between variables can be examined. Third, factorial designs do not require as many participants to obtain adequate statistical power. All three of these factors were considered when deciding what statistical analyses would most appropriately answer the first three research questions in this study.

Multiple regression procedures were used to answer the fourth research question. The fourth research question asks the following:

4. Does the combination of quality of relations with parents, gender, and level of self-esteem have a predictive relationship with the degree of internalizing problems reported by at-risk adolescents?

The literature suggests that all three variables, quality of parent relations, gender, and level of self-esteem are each related to internalizing problems separately (Kliewer et al., 2001; Kubik, et al., 2003; Marsh et al., 2004; Manders et al., 2006; Ronnlund & Karlsson, 2006). Multiple regression procedures allow the researcher to determine whether the combination variables improve the prediction of the criterion variable (Hammond, 2000; Howell, 2004). The fourth research question seeks to determine whether the combination of gender, level of self-esteem, and quality of relations with parents can better predict the level of internalizing problems than each criterion variable alone.

All four research questions were answered using existing data. The data contained in the BASC-2 electronic scoring database was specifically selected because it was taken from at-risk children and adolescents, which is the population of focus for this study. Children and adolescents that are given the BASC-2 in this particular school district are youngsters that either receive special education services as a result of an identified emotional/behavioral disorder or have been referred for a special education evaluation because an emotional/behavioral disorder is suspected. According to National Association of School Psychologists (2003) children and adolescents with emotional and behavioral disorders are at-risk for a wide variety of academic, social, vocational problems, as well as adjustment problems in adulthood.

Participant protection was an important benefit of using existing data. Specifically, no direct test administration was necessary to obtain the needed information. Care was used in designing the research plan to ensure that the data would be provided only after all identifying information was removed. These factors significantly reduced the possibility of doing harm to research participants. According to the National Commission for the Protection of Human Subjects of Research (1979), "do no harm" is an ethical principle of paramount importance that must be followed when conducting research on human participants, including their records.

Measures

In this line of research, the Achenbach System of Empirically Based Assessment (ASEBA) is a widely used research tool. In fact, the ASEBA has been used in approximately 6,000 publications to date (Achenbach, 2006). However, there are several limitations of the ASEBA that are specific to this study. First, the most recent norms on the ASEBA-YSR are over six years old. Second, this instrument does not measure self-esteem or the quality of parent-child relationships. Finally, this instrument is not used in the school district that is under study. These drawbacks were considerations that influenced the final selection of the measurement tool for this study.

The Behavior Assessment System of Children; Second Edition Self-Report of Personality (BASC-2 SRP) was chosen as the measurement tool for this study. The BASC-2 SRP is a multi-dimensional, norm-referenced, individually administered, report of personality, affect, and self-perceptions (Reynolds & Kamphaus, 2004). The BASC-2 SRP has several advantages over the ASEBA-YSR that were specific to this study. First, the BASC-2 was revised in 2004 and includes norms that are newer than the ASEBA-YSR. Second, the BASC-2 SRP includes an Internalizing Problems composite as well as a Parent Relations scale and a Self-Esteem scale. This streamlined the data collection process by eliminating the need for additional measures. Third, the BASC-2 SRP is an evaluation tool that is already administered in the school district chosen for this study. This too simplified the process of collecting data. Finally, the technical characteristics of the BASC-2 SRP are acceptable for the purpose of research.

Reynold and Kamphaus (2004) conducted several reliability studies on the BASC-2 SRP. Reliability refers to consistency of the test (Hammond, 2000). Internal consistency is quite high for the BASC-2 SRP. The internal consistency reliabilities for the composite scores ranged from the middle .80s to the middle .90s for each norm group. The internal consistency reliabilities for individual scales were slightly lower, with coefficients ranging from the middle .70s to the low .80s (2004).

Reynolds and Kamphaus (2004) also examined test-retest reliabilities for the test composites as well as individual scales. Test-retest reliability was calculated by having a selection of individuals from each age group from the original norm sample complete the same questionnaire again several weeks later. Test-retest reliability coefficients for the composite scales ranged from the upper .70s to the low .80s at the child and adolescent levels and the upper .80s to the low .90s at the college level. Similar to the internal consistency reliabilities, test-retest reliabilities for the individual scales were slightly lower, and ranged from the low .70s to the middle .80s. Nunnally (1978) suggests that

27

reliability coefficients should be at least .70 to be considered sufficient for use in research. Using this as a guide, the BASC-2 SRP can be considered a reliable test instrument for research purposes.

Reynolds and Kamphaus (2004) addressed various types of validity of the BASC-2. Validity generally refers to how well an instrument measures what it is intended to measure (Hammond, 2000). Validity was addressed by having the same children and adolescents respond to other self-report measures at the same time that they completed the BASC-2 SRP. Doing so provided correlations between the results of the two instruments, thereby providing and indication of the "degree to which they measured the same behavioral dimensions" (p. 213). The authors noted, however, that although many of the scales used in the different instruments share the same name, they may not define the construct the identically. This would lower the correlations between the two instruments and the respective scales.

One study reported by Reynolds and Kamphaus (2004) examined the inter-correlations between the BASC-2 SRP and the Achenbach System of Empirically Based Assessment-Youth Self-Report (ASEBA-YSR) (Achenbach, 1991). Participants, which included 51 adolescents ages 12-18, completed both questionnaires. Composites and scales with similar names had the following inter-correlations: Internalizing Problems and Internalizing Problems .80, Emotional Symptoms Index and Total Problems composite .75, Inattention/Hyperactivity and ADHD scale .75, Somatization and Somatic Complaints .66, Atypicality and Thought Problems .68, Anxiety and Anxious/Depressed .83, Depression and Withdrawn/Depressed .72, Social Stress and Social Problems .72, and Attention Problems .71. Overall, the composites and the scales on the BASC-2 SRP

28

and the ASEBA-YSR appear to be moderately to highly correlated, which suggests that the BASC-2 is a valid measurement tool.

Determining scale inter-correlations and factor structure is another method of measuring the validity of an instrument. Reynolds and Kamphaus (2004) used a computerized program (Amos 5.0) to assist with the statistical calculations. Specifically, if factors correlated highly, they were tested to determine if the difference between the factors was statistically significant. If they were not deemed significantly different, the scales were merged. Further, composite scales were also formed as a result of confirmatory and exploratory factor analysis (2004).

The BASC-2 SRP also incorporates several indexes that enhance the instrument's validity. These indexes were designed to evaluate the authenticity and truthfulness of the respondents' answers to each item. Reynolds and Kamphaus (2004) described each index in the following manner. The L Index addresses the possibility of a respondent "faking good" or a tendency to always answer items in a socially desirable manner. In contrast, the F Index addresses the possibility of a respondent "faking bad" or answering items in an overly negative manner. Another scale, the V Index, includes nonsense items that are used to identify carelessness, uncooperativeness, or possible reading difficulties. The Consistency Index is provided to identify conflicting responses to similar items. Each of these scales is designed to increase the likelihood of valid results (2004).

Overall, the BASC-2 SRP is an excellent tool to use to measure the variables under examination in this study. It has strong technical characteristics, updated norms, and measures all of the variables under investigation in this study. These factors, as well as the convenience of the sample, were all considered in choosing the BASC-2 as a measurement tool.

Chapter Summary

This chapter critically reviewed the relevant literature that provided the basis for the research questions of the current study. The identified gaps in the literature on internalizing problems involve three general issues. One issue is with regard to the samples used in the studies. First, many of the studies used ethnically homogeneous groups that are not generalizable beyond those specific groups. Second, many studies' conclusions were based on age ranges outside of the age range of interest in this study. Third, no studies focused specifically on the at-risk population. This supports the need for research on internalizing disorders in 8 - 18 year-old at-risk children and adolescents on a sample that is more representative of the U.S. population.

The second issue involves the instruments used to measure the internalizing problems. No studies examined internalizing problems as a single disorder; rather, individual disorders within the internalizing cluster were examined. Also, the instruments used also norms that are relatively old. Finally, each of the studies used a variety of tools to measure the variables under investigation. These limitations provide support for using the BASC-2. The BASC-2 includes all of the variable interest in one instrument, has updated norms, and measures internalizing problems as a single cluster.

The third issue involves the designs of the studies that have been conducted to date. Most of them focused on individual factors that put adolescents at-risk for internalizing problems. Few of them considered the effects of multiple variables, and no studies examined potential interactions between variables. Moreover, there were few studies that examined combinations of factors that may predict internalizing problems. By using factorial ANOVA, in combination with multiple regression, it is possible to identify potential interactions between variables as well as determine if predictive relationships exist.

CHAPTER 3. METHODOLOGY

Restatement of Purpose

This study examined whether the degree of internalizing problems in at-risk children and adolescents varies according to the quality of relations with parents, gender, and level of self-esteem as suggested in the literature (Kliewer et al., 2001; Kubik et al., 2003; Marsh et al., 2004; Manders et al., 2006; Ronnlund & Karlsson, 2006). Also investigated was whether the combination of these factors, taken together, predicts the degree of internalizing disorders reported by at-risk children and adolescents.

Research Design

This causal-comparative research study used a 2 X 2 X 2 factorial design to examine the potentially complex interactions between quality of relations with parents, gender, and level of self-esteem with the degree of internalizing problems reported by at-risk children and adolescents. Archival data was extracted from the BASC-2 Assist Plus[TM] (American Guidance Services, 2005) electronic scoring database in a public school district in northeastern Minnesota. Additional analysis was completed to determine if the quality of relations with parents, gender, and level of self-esteem play a predictive role in the degree of internalizing problems in at-risk children and adolescents.

Target Population

This study focused on at-risk children and adolescents ages 8 - 18 that attend school in a school district in northeastern Minnesota. The Minnesota Department of

Education (2005) reported demographic information for each Minnesota school for the 2005 - 2006 school year. According to the most recent demographic information provided by the Minnesota Department of Education (2005), the school district used in this study is comprised of 10,429 students. The ethnic composition is White 86%, African American 5%, American Indian 5%, Asian 2%, and Hispanic 1%. Thirty-eight percent of students qualify for free and reduced lunch, 12% of the student population receives special education services, and 0% of students are considered Limited English Proficient (2005).

Selection of Documents

This study uses archived BASC-2 records from the BASC-2 ASSIST Plus [TM] electronic scoring database from a public school district in northeastern Minnesota. Using the statistical program G*Power 2.0 (Faul & Erdfelder, 1992), a total sample of 252 records was needed to complete a factorial ANOVA with three groups. This sample size was calculated based on alpha .05, power .95, and effect size .25 (1992). Test records that contained an Extreme Caution score on any of the validity indexes embedded within the BASC-2 were eliminated from the sample.

Definition of Variables

There are three independent variables and one dependent variable included in this study. The independent variables include quality of relations with parents, gender, and level of self-esteem. The dependent variable is degree of internalizing problems. To address the first three research questions, 2 X 2 X 2 factorial ANOVA will be used.

Factorial ANOVA requires that the independent variables be nominal; in other words, they must differ by category (Howell, 2004). The dependent variable must at least be at the interval level (2004). Therefore, the variables are defined as follows:

IV_1 - Quality of relations with parents was measured according to two levels. The Average/Above Average (AV/AA) Parent Relations group represents the youngsters that display average or better quality relationships with their parents. In contrast, the At-Risk/Clinically Significant (AR/CS) Parent Relations group represents youngsters that display problems in their relationships with their parents.

IV_2 - Gender was recorded as Male or Female, obtained from the demographic information section of the BASC-2.

IV_3 - Level of self-esteem were measured according to two levels. The Average/Above Average (AV/AA) Self-Esteem group represents children and adolescents with average or better self-esteem. In contrast, the At-Risk/Clinically Significant (AR/CS) Self-Esteem group represents the children and adolescents that display mild to significant problems with low self-esteem.

DV - Degree of internalizing problems was measured by the obtained T-score on the BASC-2 on the Internalizing Problems scale.

Stepwise multiple regression procedures were used to answer the fourth research question. Thus, the three independent variables, as well as the dependent variable must be defined at least at an interval level (Howell, 2004). Although survey data is technically considered ordinal (Fife-Shaw, 2000), it is often treated as interval level in psychological research (Howell, 2004). In the case that the variable is categorical, it may be "dummy

34

coded" and entered into the regression formula. Thus, the variables were defined as the following:

IV$_1$ - Quality of relations with parents was measured as to the obtained T-score on the Relations with Parents scale on the BASC-2.

IV$_2$ - Gender was recorded as Male or Female, as obtained on the demographic information section of the BASC-2. Gender was "dummy coded" so that it could be entered into the regression formula. Males were assigned 1 and Females were assigned 2.

IV$_3$ - Level of self-esteem was measured as the obtained T-score on the Self-Esteem scale on the BASC-2.

DV - Degree of internalizing problems was measured as the obtained T-score on the Internalizing Problems scale on the BASC-2.

Instruments

All variables were obtained from BASC-2 test records that are archived the BASC-2 ASSIST Plus^{TM} electronic scoring database a public school district in northeastern Minnesota. The BASC-2 is a multi-dimensional, multi-method, norm-referenced, individually administered, report of personality, affect, and self-perceptions (Reynolds & Kamphaus, 2004). Eighteen primary scales are included in the BASC-2 Self-Report of Personality; however, this study utilizes only the Relations with Parents, Self-Esteem and Internalizing Problems. Gender is identified by the demographic information collected on the BASC-2.

Data Collection and Procedures

This project began after the Capella University Human Subjects Institutional Review Board (IRB) as well as the Superintendent and Director of Special Services from the Duluth Public Schools granted permission to proceed. All procedures outlined in the IRB application were strictly followed.

As noted earlier, the data needed for this project is stored in the BASC-2 ASSIST Plus [TM] electronic scoring database in a school district in northeastern Minnesota. Specific employees including the Special Services Business Manager, the Special Services Technology Support Personnel, and the Special Services Department secretaries manage the database. Once permission was obtained, the Special Services Business Manager exported all of the BASC-2 data to a Microsoft Excel spreadsheet. The columns that contained student names and student identification numbers were deleted from the spreadsheet. After all of the identifying information was deleted from the spreadsheet, the remaining data was saved electronically and was sent to the researcher's password protected work email account. At that point, the researcher deleted the data files that met the exclusionary criterion (records that contained an Extreme Caution designation on any of the validity indexes). The remaining data was saved electronically.

Although the data did not contain any identifying information, additional safeguards were in place for storing the data. Specifically, the electronic data file was saved unto the researcher's password protected laptop computer. A back-up copy was saved unto a data storage compact disc and was locked in a file cabinet at the researcher's work office. Upon completion of the study, or in the event that the researcher changes employment, the data file will be deleted from the researcher's work laptop computer.

The compact disc will also be moved from the locked file cabinet at the researcher's work office to another locked file cabinet at the researcher's home office for the remainder of the required seven years post-publication. Only the researcher has a key for either file cabinet. At the end of the seven-year period, the compact disc will be destroyed and disposed in the trash.

Research Questions and Hypotheses

This study seeks to answer four research questions. Each research question, followed by the corresponding hypothesis set, is as follows.

1. Research Question: Is there a statistically significant difference in the degree of internalizing problems between the two Relations with Parents groups (Average/ Above Average and At-Risk/Clinically Significant) as measured by the BASC-2?

   Null Hypothesis: There will not be a statistically significant difference in the degree of internalizing problems between the two Relations with Parents groups (Average/Above Average and At-Risk/Clinically Significant) as measured by the BASC-2.

   Alternative Hypothesis: There will be a statistically significant difference in the degree of internalizing problems between the two Relations with Parents groups (Average/Above Average and At-Risk/Clinically Significant) at the .05 level, as measured by the BASC-2.

2. Research Question: Is there a statistically significant difference in the degree of internalizing problems between the two gender groups (Male and Female) as measured by the BASC-2?

Null Hypothesis: There will not be a statistically significant difference in the degree of internalizing problems between the two gender groups (Male and Female) as measured by the BASC-2.

Alternative Hypothesis: There will be a statistically significant difference in the degree of internalizing problems between the two gender groups (Male and Female) at the .05 level, as measured by the BASC-2.

3. Research Question: Is there a statistically significant difference in the degree of internalizing problems between the two Self-Esteem groups (Average/Above Average, and At-Risk/Clinically Significant) as measured by the BASC-2?
   Null Hypothesis: There will not be a statistically significant difference in the degree of internalizing problems between the two Self-Esteem groups (Average/Above Average, and At-Risk/Clinically Significant) as measured by the BASC-2.

   Alternative Hypothesis: There will be a statistically significant difference in the degree of internalizing problems between the two Self-Esteem groups (Average/Above Average and At-Risk/Clinically Significant) at the .05 level, as measured by the BASC-2.

4. Research Question: Does the combination of quality of relations with parents, gender, and level of self-esteem have a predictive relationship with the degree of internalizing problems reported by at-risk children and adolescents?

Null Hypothesis: The combination of the quality of relations with parents, gender, and level of self-esteem will not have a predictive relationship with the degree of internalizing problems reported by at-risk children and adolescents.

Alternative Hypothesis: The combination of the quality of relations with parents, gender, and level of self-esteem will have a predictive relationship with the degree of internalizing problems reported by at-risk children and adolescents.

Data Analysis

The anonymous data resulting from the data collection procedures was entered into the Statistical Program for the Social Sciences (SPSS) version 13.0 for Windows (SPSS, 2004). To test the first three null hypotheses, the data was transformed from T-scores to categories based on the criteria described in *Definition of Terms*. This was done so that factorial ANOVA could be used to analyze the data. Quality of parent relations and level of self-esteem was categorized as Average/Above Average (AV/AA) and At-Risk/Clinically Significant (AR/CS); Gender was entered as Male or Female. The obtained T-scores on the Internalizing Problems scale were also recorded. After the data was entered into SPSS, factorial ANOVA was used to detect significant differences between the three factors at each level and the degree of internalizing problems. Main effects and simple effects for relations with parents, gender, and self-esteem were examined.

Next, the fourth null hypothesis was tested. Thus, the predictor and criterion variables were entered in a manner that multiple regression procedures can be used. Specifically, quality of relations with parents, level of self-esteem, and degree of

39

internalizing problems was entered as the T-scores obtained on the respective scales on the BASC-2. Gender was "dummy coded" as Male 1 and Female 2. After the data is entered, inter-correlations between the predictor variables were computed to determine if significant multicollinearilty exists; if the predictor variables are highly correlated, the obtained results may not generalize from one sample to another (Howell, 2004). Finally, multiple regression analysis was used to determine whether the quality of relations with parents, gender, and the level of self-esteem have a predictive relationship with internalizing problems.

Expected Findings

The literature suggests that there will be statistically significant main effects between the degree of internalizing problems and the two parent relations groups, the degree of internalizing problems and the two gender groups, as well as the degree of internalizing problems and the two self-esteem groups (Kliewer et al., 2001; Kubik et al., 2003; Marsh, et al., 2004; Manders et al., 2006; Ronnlund & Karlsson, 2006). Specifically, it is anticipated that the results will support the idea that adolescents with poor quality relationships with their parents (At-Risk/Clinically Significant) will report a higher degree of internalizing problems than those with average or better quality parent relations (Average/Above Average), regardless of gender and level of self-esteem. It is also anticipated that female adolescents will report a higher degree of internalizing problems than males, regardless of the quality of relations with parents and level of self-esteem. Finally, it is expected that adolescents with a low level of self-esteem (At-Risk/Clinically Significant) will report a higher degree of internalizing problems than those

40

with a high level of self-esteem (Average/Above Average), regardless of the quality of parent relations and gender.

Because no research to date has explored the potential interactions between and among the quality of parent relations, gender, level of self-esteem, and degree of internalizing problems, it is unknown whether simple effects will exist between the stated variables. It is also unknown whether the quality of relations with parents, gender, and self-esteem will have a predictive relationship with internalizing problems in at-risk adolescents, because research is also lacking in this area. However, if a predictive relationship exists, practitioners will be able to target certain groups for intervention prior to the development of internalizing disorders and the problems often associated with these disorders.

CHAPTER 4. RESULTS

Organization of Chapter

This chapter presents the results of the descriptive and inferential statistical analyses that were conducted on the collected data. The first section describes the overall characteristics of the sample. The second section tests the first three null hypotheses using factorial ANOVA. Also included in this section is an examination of the data as well as a verification of the assumptions of ANOVA. The third section tests the fourth null hypothesis using multiple regression procedures, including data screening and verification of the corresponding assumptions. Finally, the last section of the chapter concludes with a summary of relevant findings.

Characteristics of the Sample

The data collected for this study was from at-risk 8 - 18 year olds that attend public school in northeastern Minnesota. There were 256 cases available for analysis in the BASC-2 electronic database. However, 4 of the cases were eliminated from the sample as a result of Extreme Caution scores reported on one or more of the validity indexes embedded within the BASC-2. This resulted in a total sample of 252 cases, of which 65 were females and 187 were males. Mean Scores, standard deviations, and sample size for each variable is presented in Table 1. Table 2 shows mean scores, standard deviations, and the sample size of the possible variable combinations.

42

Table 1. Descriptive Statistics of Each Group

	Mean	Standard Deviation	N
Internalizing Problems	54.77	11.608	252
Parent Relations	44.43	11.233	252
Gender	1.26	.438	252
Self-Esteem	47.48	12.097	252

Note: N = number of participants

Table 2. Descriptive Statistics for Internalizing Problems at Each Variable Combination

Gender	Parent Relations	Self-Esteem	Mean*	Standard Deviation	N
Female	AV/AA	AV/AA	53.09	11.151	32
		AR/CS	62.33	16.293	6
		Total	54.55	12.317	38
	AR/CS	AV/AA	59.40	10.514	15
		AR/CS	67.42	10.518	12
		Total	62.96	11.082	27
	Total	AV/AA	55.11	11.237	47
		AR/CS	65.72	12.480	18
		Total	58.05	12.452	65
Male	AV/AA	AV/AA	49.49	8.885	113
		AR/CS	62.20	6.197	10
		Total	50.52	9.353	123
	AR/CS	AV/AA	53.94	10.320	36
		AR/CS	66.93	9.459	28
		Total	59.63	11.818	64
	Total	AV/AA	50.56	9.413	149
		AR/CS	65.68	8.893	38
		Total	53.64	11.111	187
Total	AV/AA	AV/AA	50.28	9.509	145
		AR/CS	62.65	10.561	16
		Total	51.47	10.234	161
	AR/CS	AV/AA	55.55	10.574	51
		AR/CS	67.08	9.654	40
		Total	60.62	11.645	91
	Total	AV/AA	51.65	10.041	196
		AR/CS	65.70	10.067	56
		Total	54.77	11.608	252

Note: AV/AA = Average to Above Average; AR/CS = At-Risk to Clinically Significant.
* Internalizing Problems Mean = 54.77

Testing Null Hypotheses 1, 2, and 3

Data Screening and Verification of Assumptions

The first three research questions were answered by testing the null hypotheses

using factorial ANOVA. ANOVA requires the consideration of five assumptions, which include random sampling, interval or ratio measurement for the dependent variable, normally distributed groups, equal variance between groups (homoscedasticity), and absence of outliers. Each of these assumptions was systematically examined.

Random Sampling.

Random sampling is necessary to make accurate interpretations of the data (Howell, 2004). Using the statistical program G*Power 2.0 (Faul & Erdfelder, 1992), it was determined that a total sample of 252 records were needed to complete a factorial ANOVA with three groups, based on alpha .05, power .95, and effect size .25. Because there was a total of 256 data files available in the BASC-2 database, the total population was sampled. Therefore, this assumption was met.

Interval or Ratio Scaled Dependent Variable.

At least an interval level dependent variable is necessary in order to complete parametric procedures (Howell, 2004). The dependent variable in this study, level of Internalizing Problems, was measured as the obtained T-score on the BASC-2. There is some debate among researchers whether scores obtained from questionnaires should be considered ordinal or interval (Fife-Schaw, 2000). However, for practical purposes, most survey data is treated as interval scaled in psychological research (2004). This assumption was also met.

Normal Distribution.

Univariate procedures assume that each variable is normally distributed. Table 3 presents the data necessary for this analysis. According to Field (2005), skewness and kurtosis values of zero indicate a normal distribution. Results indicated that the data has a moderate positive skew; kurtosis is slight. The histogram in Figure 1 illustrates the

positive skewness of the data as well as slight kurtosis.

Table 3. Skewness and Kurtosis of Internalizing Problems

	N	Mean	Skewness	Standard Error	Kurtosis	Standard Error
Internalizing Problems	252	54.77	.738	.153	.148	.306

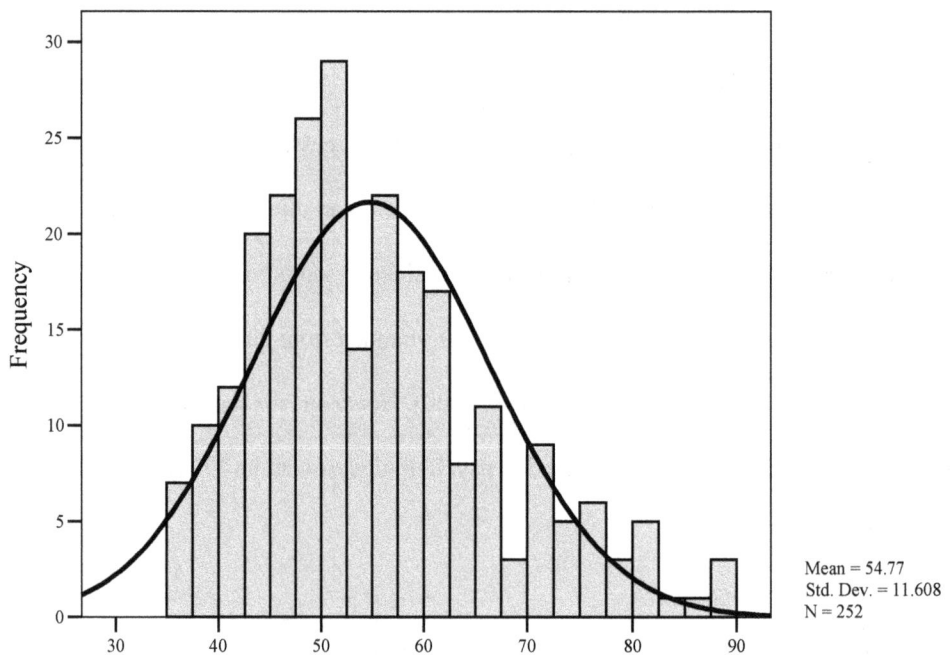

Figure 1. Histogram of mean internalizing problems scores

Preliminary analysis of the data suggested that the assumption of normality was questionable for this sample and that additional tests of normality were warranted. Table 4 presents the outcomes of two statistical tests of the normality assumption. Both the Kolmogorov-Smirnov and the Shapiro-Wilk tests of normality were significant ($p =$ .000). This indicates that the normality assumption was violated. It is not surprising that the mean of this sample is higher than the mean of the standardization sample of the BASC-2 (54.77 vs. 50), because the focus of this study is at-risk adolescents who either have an emotional or behavioral disability or were suspected of having one.

Table 4. Tests of Normality on the Dependent Variable Internalizing Problems

	Kolmogorov-Smirnov[a]			Shapiro-Wilk		
	Statistic	df	p	Statistic	df	p
Internalizing Problems	.094	252	.000	.956	252	.000

Note: df = degrees of freedom, p = degree of significance, [a] Lilliefors significance correction.

Equal Variances (Homoscedasticity)

Next, Levene's test was used to determine the tenability of the assumption of equal variances (homoscedasticity). The results of Levene's test are presented in Table 5. Results indicated that between group variance was not significant ($p = .333$). Thus, the assumption of homogeneity was met.

Table 5. Levene's Test of Equality of Error Variances for Internalizing Problems

F	df1	df2	p
1.150	7	244	.333

Note: df = degrees of freedom, p = degree of significance.

Absence of Outliers.

Finally, the data was examined for outliers. Figures 2, 3, and 4 present the plots of Internalizing Problems scores by Parent Relations, Gender, and Self-Esteem groups. Three outliers were present within the Average/Above Average (AV/AA) Parent Relations group. Specifically, Internalizing Problems values were much higher for three children and adolescents with Average to Above Average (AV/AA) Self-Esteem. For the variable Gender, two outliers were identified within the group of Males. Two Males reported much greater Internalizing Problems in comparison to the others in the sample. The Average/Above Average (AV/AA) Self-Esteem group also had outliers in terms of Internalizing Problems. Specifically, 6 children and adolescents within the Average/Above Average (AV/AA) group reported Internalizing Problems much higher than others within the Average/Above Average (AV/AA) Self-Esteem group.

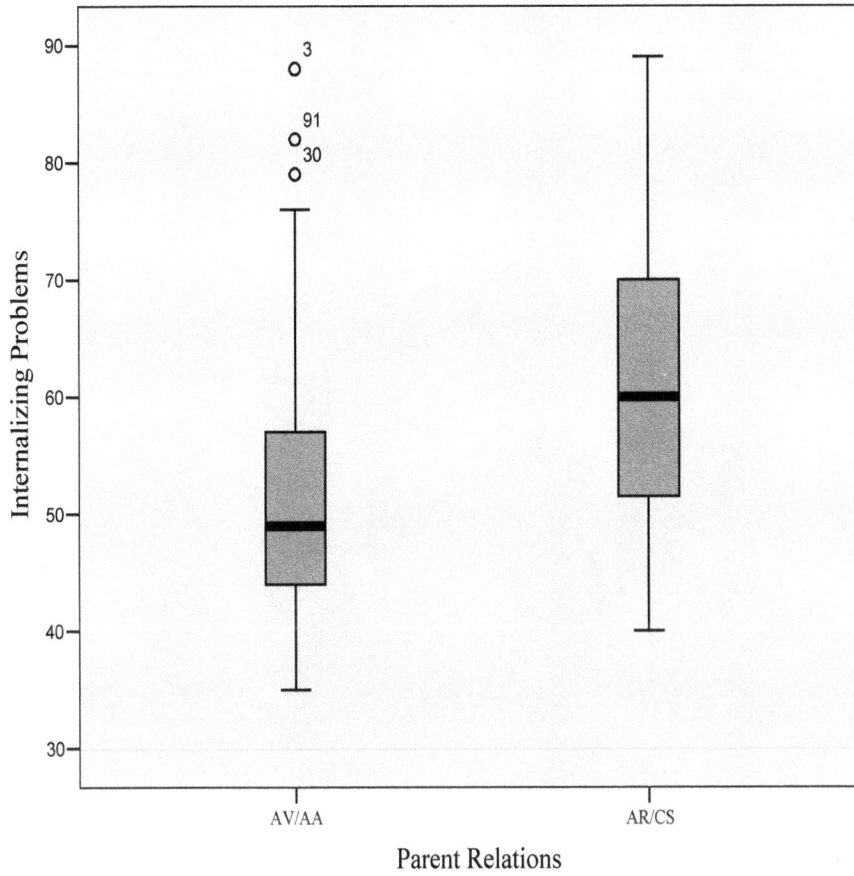

Figure 2. Box plot of internalizing problems by parent relations groups

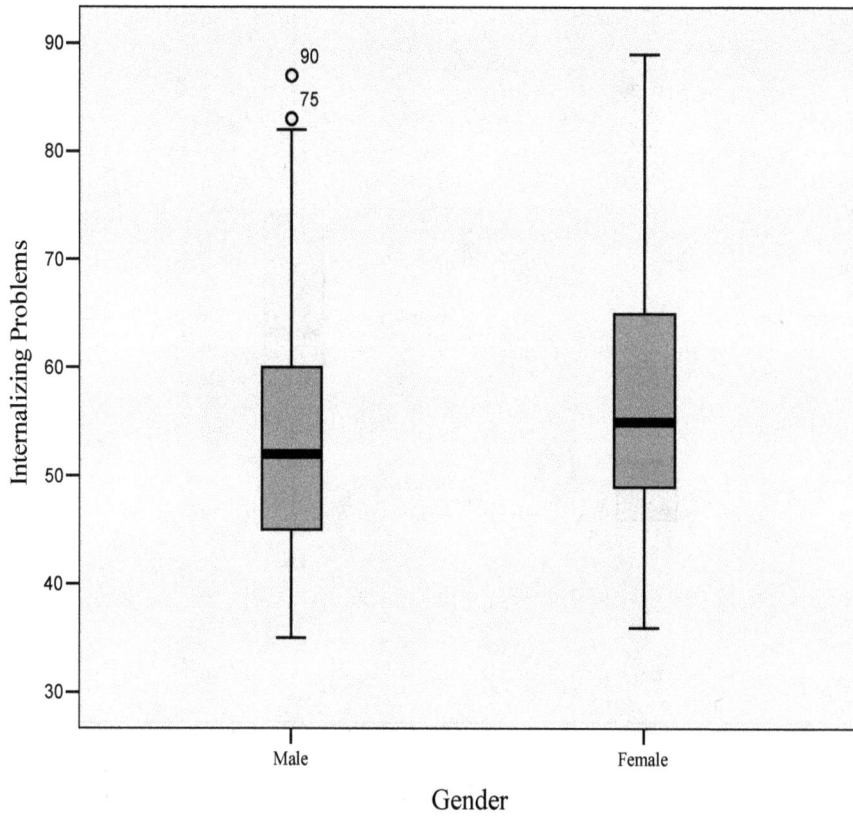

Figure 3. Box plot of internalizing problems by gender

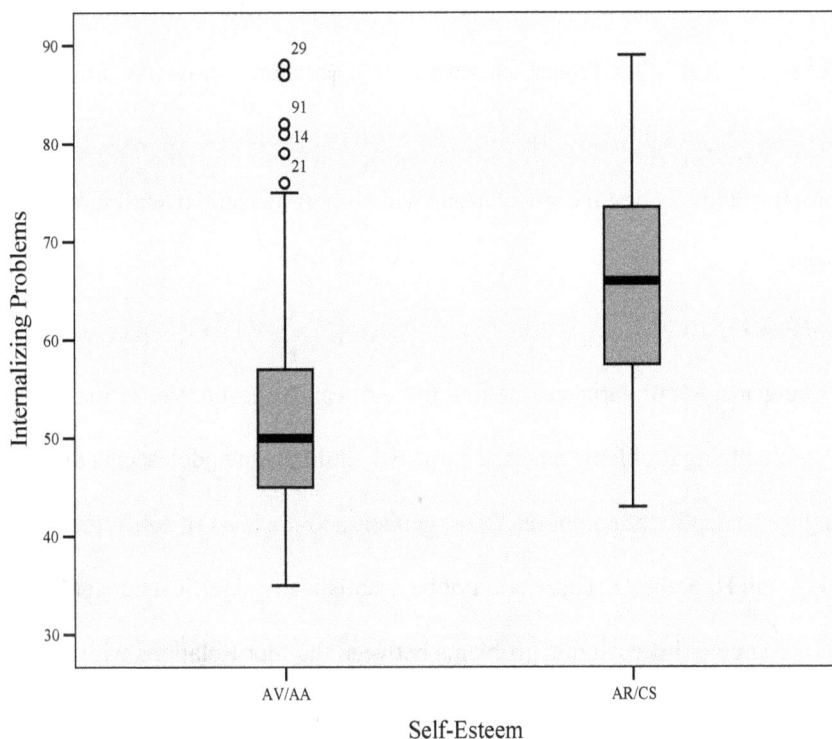

Figure 4. Box plot of internalizing problems by self-esteem group

Summary of Assumptions

There are five assumptions that must be examined when conducting analysis of variance. An examination of the data revealed that the assumptions of random sampling, a ratio or interval level dependent variable, and homoscedasticity were met. However, the assumption of normality was violated, and outliers were present in all three independent variables.

Although the assumption of normality was not met and outliers were present within the data, Howell (2004) asserts that ANOVA is "robust against violations of

51

assumptions" (p. 367). Specifically, if the "populations are either symmetric or at least similar in shape" and "if the largest variance is no more than four or five times the smallest" the results of the analysis of variance can be considered valid (p. 383). Therefore, it is unlikely that these violations will compromise the overall interpretation of these results.

Results of ANOVA

Using analysis of variance, the first three research questions examine whether the level of Internalizing Problems reported by at-risk children and adolescents differ according to the quality of parent relations, gender, and the level of self-esteem.

1. Null Hypothesis: There will not be a statistically significant difference in the degree of internalizing problems between the four Relations with Parents groups (Average/Above Average and At-Risk/Clinically Significant) as measured by the BASC-2.

2. Null Hypothesis: There will not be a statistically significant difference in the degree of internalizing problems between the two gender groups (Male and Female) as measured by the BASC-2.

3. Null Hypothesis: There will not be a statistically significant difference in the degree of internalizing problems between the four Self-Esteem groups (Average/Above Average and At-Risk/Clinically Significant) as measured by the BASC-2.

A 2 x 2 x 2 factorial ANOVA was used to test each of the hypotheses; the results are presented in Table 6. An examination of the results revealed significant main effects for Parent Relations [F (1, 244) = 8.530] and Self-Esteem [F (1, 244) = 37.173]. As a

52

result, the first and third null hypotheses can be rejected. In contrast, no significant main effect for Gender was found $[F(1, 244) = 1.889]$. Thus, the second null must be retained. Finally, there were no significant interactions between Gender x Parent Relations $[F(1, 244) = .098]$. Gender x Self-Esteem $[F(1, 244) = 1.436]$, Parent Relations x Self-Esteem $[F(1, 244) = .018]$, or Gender x Parent Relations x Self-Esteem $[F(1, 244) = .045]$. Figure 5 graphically depicts the results of the ANOVA.

Table 6. Analysis of Variance for Internalizing Problems

Source	df	F	p	Partial Eta Squared	Observed Power[a]
Parent Relations	1	8.530	.004	.034	.829
Gender	1	1.886	.171	.008	.278
Self-Esteem	1	37.173	.000	.132	1.00
Parent Relations x Gender	1	.098	.755	.000	.061
Parent Relations x Self-Esteem	1	.018	.893	.000	.052
Gender x Self-Esteem	1	1.436	.232	.006	.222
Parent Relations x Gender x Self-Esteem	1	.045	.832	.000	.055
Error	244	(95.402)			

Note: df = degrees of freedom, F = F statistic, p = degree of significance, [a] = computed using alpha = .05.

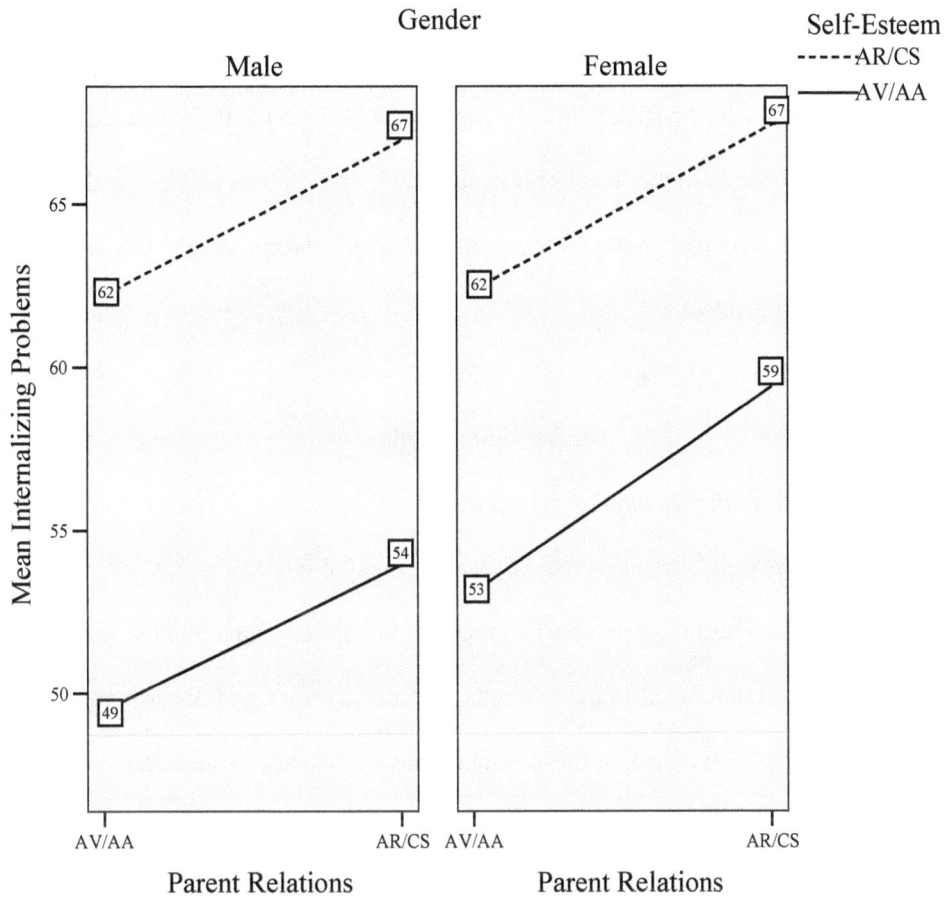

Figure 5. Results of Analysis of Variance

The data indicates that the level of internalizing problems experienced by at-risk children and adolescents differed depending on the quality of relations they have with their parents. Specifically, children and adolescents with At-Risk/Clinically Significant (AR/CS) Parent Relations reported a higher level of internalizing problems than children and adolescents with Average/Above Average (AV/AA) Parent Relations. This was the case for both genders. In addition, the level of internalizing problems experienced by at-risk children and adolescents differed depending on their reported level of self-esteem; specifically, those with At-Risk/Clinically Significant (AR/CS) Self-Esteem experienced reported a significantly higher level of Internalizing Problems than children and adolescents with Average/Above Average (AV/AA) Self-Esteem. Again, this pattern was consistent across genders.

Testing Null Hypothesis 4

Data Screening and Verification of Assumptions

The fourth null hypothesis will be tested using multiple regression procedures. Multiple regression also requires consideration of assumptions. Quantitative variables, no mulitcollinearity, homoscedasticity, normally distributed errors, and linearity must be considered (Field, 2005). Each of these assumptions was closely examined.

Quantitative Variables.

The first assumption is that the predictor and criterion variables must be quantitative. The predictor variables, Parent Relations and Self-Esteem were measured as T-scores. Gender was dummy coded (Male = 1, Female = 2). The criterion variable, Internalizing Problems, was also measured as a T-score. Each of the variables of the study is quantitative; thus, the assumption of quantitative variables was met.

No Multicollinearity.

The data was examined for multicollinearity using the Pearson Correlation. Table 7 presents the results of this analysis. An examination of the predictor variables indicates that Gender and Self-Esteem correlate significantly ($r = .167$, $p < .05$), as does Parent

56

Relations and Self-Esteem ($r = .452, p < .01$). However, both coefficients are relatively small. This suggests that each variable is measuring something different and that multicollinearity is minimal.

Table 7. Correlations Between Variables

		Internalizing Problems	Parent Relations	Gender	Self-Esteem
Pearson Correlation	Internalizing Problems	1.00	-.411	.167	-.626
	Parent Relations	-.411	—	-.012	.452
	Gender	.167	-.012	—	-.127
	Self-Esteem	-.626	.452	-.127	—
p (1-tailed)	Internalizing Problems	—	.000	.004	.000
	Parent Relations	.000	—	.425	.000
	Gender	.004	.425	—	.000

Further examination confirms this assumption. Table 8 shows the results of collinearity diagnostics. According to Field (2005), for the assumption of no multicollinearity to be met, Variance Inflation Factor (VIF) values must be less than 1. In addition, if the VIF is close to 1, multicollinearity can be ruled out (2005). Further,

57

Menard (1995) argues that tolerance values below .2 indicate potential multicollinearity. Examination of Table 8 confirms that there is not significant collinearity between the independent variables; therefore, this assumption was met.

Table 8. Summary of Variables Not Yet Entered Into the Regression Model

Model	Excluded Variables	Beta In	t	p	Partial Correlation	Collinearity Statistics	
						Tolerance	VIF
1	Parent Relations	-.409[a]	-7.184	.000	-.414	1.00	1.00
	Self-Esteem	-.615[a]	.000	.000	-.619	.984	1.016
2	Self-Esteem	-.539[b]	-9.873	.000	-.531	.781	1.281

Note: [a] Predictors in the model (Constant), Gender
[b] Predictors in the model (Constant), Gender, Parent Relations

Homoscedasticity and Linearity

The assumptions of homoscedasticity and linearity were considered in Figure 6. Figure 6 shows the plot of standardized residuals against standardized predicted values. Points are evenly dispersed and appear random, which indicates that the homoscedasticity and linearity assumptions were met (Field, 2005).

Dependent Variable: Internalizing Problems

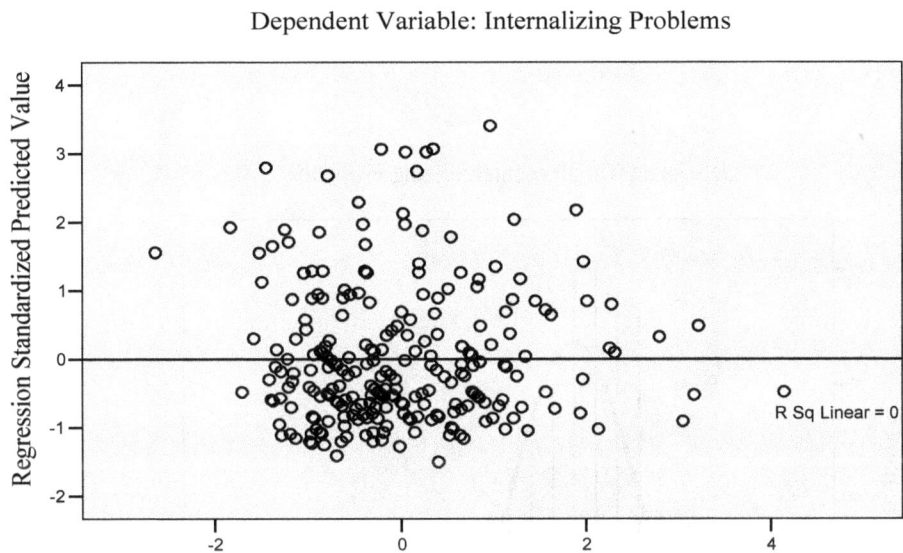

Figure 6. Scatter plot of standardized residuals by standardized predicted values

Normally Distributed Residuals

Normality of residuals assumption can be examined in Figures 7 and 8. Figure 7 shows a

histogram of the residuals. This histogram roughly mirrors the shape of the normal distribution. Figure 8 shows a straight line that also represents a normal distribution of residual errors. The assumption of normally distributed residuals was met.

Dependent Variable: Internalizing Problems

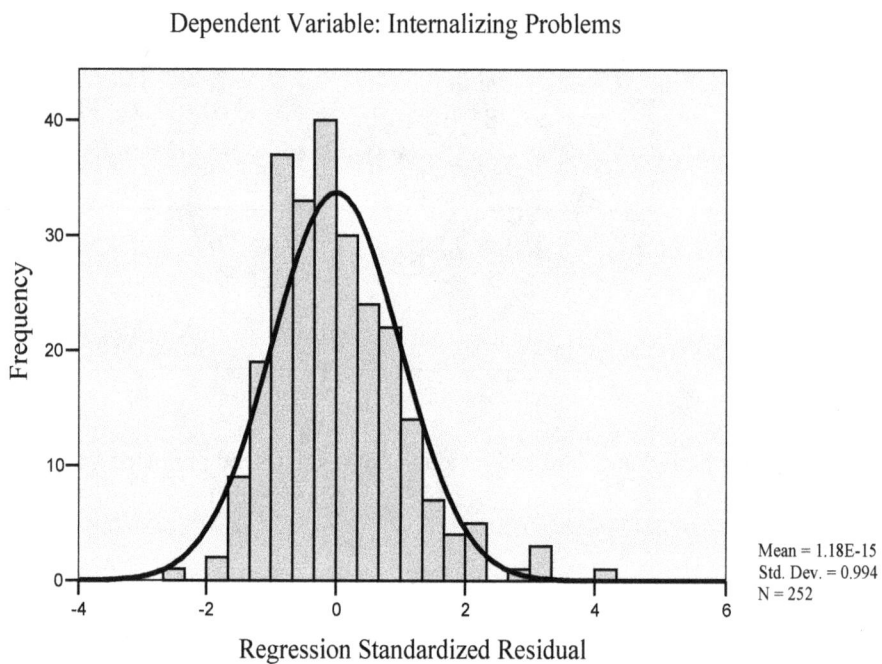

Figure 7. Histogram of standardized residuals. Line signifies a normal distribution.

Dependent Variable: Internalizing Problems

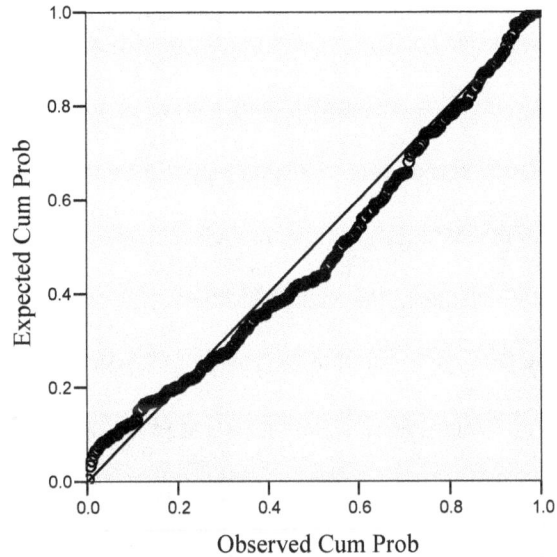

Figure 8. Plot of residual values. Straight line represents a normal distribution.

Summary of Assumptions

There are several assumptions to consider when conducting multiple regression analysis. The assumptions of quantitative variables, non-mulitcollinearity, homoscedasticity, normality of residuals, and linearity were all examined. Analyses indicated that each of the assumptions was met. As a result, it can be assumed that the regression model used in this study will be generalizable.

Results of Multiple Regression

The fourth research question examines whether the combination of quality of parent relations, gender, and the level of self-esteem can together predict the level of internalizing problems reported by at-risk children and adolescents.

4. Null Hypothesis: The combination of the quality of relations with parents, gender, and level of self-esteem does not have a predictive relationship with the degree of internalizing problems reported by at-risk adolescents.

Table 9 shows the statistics for three models. Model 1 shows that Gender alone explained 2.8% of the variance in the change in Internalizing Problems scores. This model is significantly better at predicting Internalizing Problems scores than no model at all ($R^2 = .028$, $p < .01$). When Parent Relations is added to the model (Model 2), the two variables combined explain 19.5% of the variance in the change of Internalizing Problems ($R^2 = .195$). The addition of Parent Relations accounted for a change of 16.7% and was statistically significant ($p < .01$). Finally, Model 3 examined Gender, Parent Relations, and Self-Esteem and their combined ability to predict Internalizing Problems. This combination of variables explained 42.2% of the variance in Internalizing Problems ($R^2 = .422$). Adding Self-Esteem to the model resulted in a 22.7% change, which was also statistically significant ($p < .01$). This indicated that the combination of the quality of parent relations, gender, and the level of self-esteem predicted internalizing problems in at-risk children and adolescents in this sample. Thus, null hypothesis 4 was rejected.

Table 9. Summary of Stepwise Regression Analysis for Variables Predicting Internalizing Problems ($N = 252$)

Model	R	R^2	R^2 Change	Change Statistics					Durbin-Watson
				F Change	$df\,1$	$df\,2$	Sig. F Change		
1	.167	.028	.028	7.131	1	250	.008		
2	.441	.195	.167	51.616	1	249	.000		
3	.650	.422	.227	97.485	1	248	.000		1.805

Note: Model 1 Predictors: (Constant), Gender
Model 2 Predictors: (Constant), Gender, Parent Relations
Model 3 Predictors: (Constant), Gender, Parent Relations, Self-Esteem

Table 10, Analysis of Variance, provides additional support to the rejection of null hypothesis 4. The ANOVA in Model 3 tests the null hypothesis that there is no correlation between Parent Relations, Grade, and Self-Esteem taken together with Internalizing Problems. The null hypothesis was rejected as a result of this analysis ($F = 60.33, p < .01$) and supports that Internalizing Problems are better predicted by the combination of Parent Relations, Gender, and Self-Esteem than by chance alone. Finally, Figure 9 displays a 3-dimensional image of the results of the multiple regression.

Table 10. Analysis of Variance, Change in Internalizing Problems

	Sum of Squares	df	Mean Square	F	p
Regression	14269.888	3	4756.629	60.333	.000
Residual	19552.220	248	78.840		
Total	33822.107	251			

Note: Predictors (Constant), Parent Relations, Gender, Self-Esteem

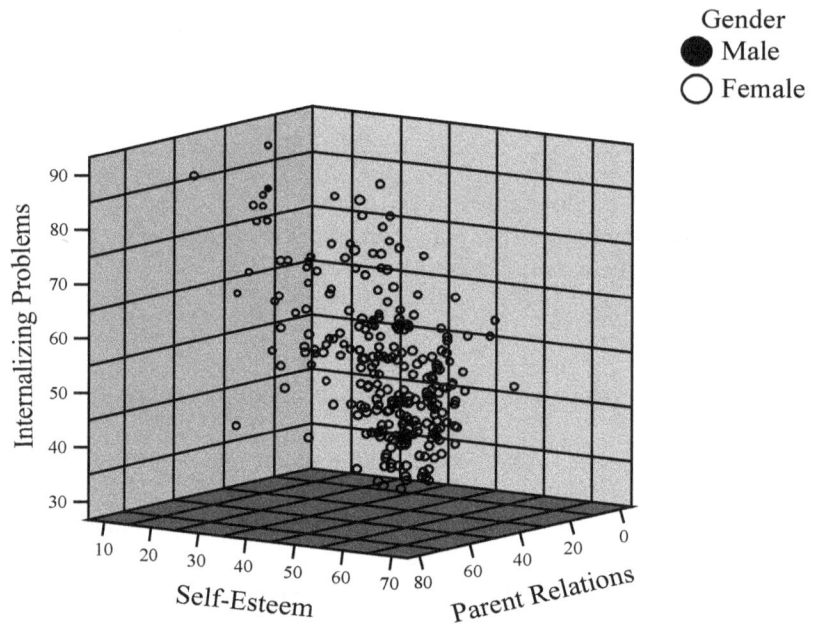

Figure 9. Visual depiction of multiple regression results.

Summary of Results

This chapter sought to answer the four research questions of this study by testing

each null hypothesis. Null hypotheses 1, 3, and 4 were rejected and were consistent with

the researcher's expectations. Specifically, the level of internalizing problems reported by

at-risk children and adolescents differed according to the quality of relationships they

reported with their parents, as well as by the reported level of self-esteem. Contrary to

expectations, however, null hypothesis 2 was accepted. There was not a statistically significant difference in the level of internalizing problems reported by males and

females. These findings, as well as the implications of these findings, will be thoroughly

discussed in Chapter 5.

CHAPTER 5. DISCUSSION

Organization of the Chapter

This final chapter is comprised of six sections. The first section provides a general overview of the study, including a brief summary of the results. The second section consists of a discussion and interpretation of findings. The discussion will systematically address each research question individually and will include an interpretation of results, how the results converge or diverge from the existing literature, as well as the implications of the findings. The third and fourth sections discuss the strengths and limitations of this study. Recommendations for future research are given in the fifth section. The last section concludes with a summary.

Overview of the Results

The purpose of this study was to examine whether girls experience a higher degree of internalizing problems in comparison to boys, and whether the lack of quality relationships with parents and low self-esteem are associated with a higher degree of internalizing problems. In addition, this study sought to investigate whether any of these factors or combination of factors, have a predictive relationship with internalizing problems. The intent was to build upon the existing understanding of internalizing disorders as they relate to at-risk children and adolescents.

Data was obtained from the BASC-2 electronic database at a public school district in northeastern Minnesota. Factorial ANOVA was used to determine whether differences in the degree of internalizing problems existed according to the quality of relations with parents, gender, and level of self-esteem. Multiple regression procedures were used to determine if a predictive relationship existed between these factors and internalizing problems.

Noteworthy findings emerged as a result of this study. First, consistent with previous research, the degree of internalizing problems differed based on the quality of parent relationships and level of self-esteem. Specifically, children and adolescents with poor parent relationships reported a higher degree of internalizing problems; those with low self-esteem also experienced a higher degree of internalizing problems. However, contrary to previous research, this study did not detect any significant gender differences in the degree of internalizing problems. Third, gender, quality of parent relationships, and level of self-esteem each predicted the level of internalizing problems. Specifically, being female predicted a higher degree of internalizing problems, as did poor relationships with parents, and low self-esteem. Further, the combination of gender, quality of relations with parents, and self-esteem significantly strengthened the prediction of internalizing problems.

Discussion and Interpretation of Findings

Research Question 1

The first research question asked whether the degree of internalizing problems is related to the quality of the parent-child relationship. The results indicated that the degree of internalizing problems reported did in fact vary according to the quality of the relationship between the child/adolescent and the parents. Specifically, children and adolescents with poor relationships with their parents reported a higher degree of

67

internalizing problems than those with average or better parent relationships. Likewise, children and adolescents with average or better quality relationships with their parents reported a lower degree of internalizing problems.

These results are consistent with the existing literature. Margolin (2006) found that internalizing problems, such as depression, social anxiety, and loneliness were negatively correlated with parent support. Manders et al. (2006) used multiple regression analysis to determine that higher quality father-adolescent and mother-adolescent relationships were related to a significantly lower level of internalizing problems. In a longitudinal study, Delaney (1996) found that youth who reported Detached relationships with their parents (high autonomy, low closeness) reported significantly higher symptoms of depression and anxiety than those who reported Connected relationships (low autonomy, high closeness) or Individuated relationships (moderate to high autonomy, high closeness) with their parents. These differences were consistent across time.

The existing studies used samples that differed from the present study. The study by Margolin (2006) was conducted solely with 6th grade African American children; Manders et al. (2006) studied 11-18 year old Dutch youth. Delaney (1996) focused on 11-13 year-olds. Each of these studies used a wide array of instruments to measure the variables; each defined the variables slightly different.

Although the demographic characteristics, measurement tools, and designs of these studies differed from this study, the results were consistent. This indicates that the present study's findings extends previous findings and provides credibility to the notion that parent-child relationships and internalizing problems are related, regardless of age, ethnicity, and measurement tools used.

These findings underscore the importance of the parent-child relationship, and suggest that good parent-child relationships may provide a protective quality to internalizing problems. This provides support for early efforts to promote healthy parent-child relationships. Information on developing healthy relationships could be disseminated by targeting schools, doctor's offices, social services, churches, and the like.

Research Question 2

The second research question asked whether there is a difference in the degree of internalizing problems between boys and girls. The results of this study did not show a difference in the degree of internalizing problems reported by boys and girls. This finding runs contrary to the existing literature. In a meta-analysis of over 20 cross-sectional studies, Leadbeater et al. (1995) reported significant gender differences in depressive symptoms after puberty. Kubik et al. (2003) also reported significant gender differences in depressive symptoms in 12 - 13 year-olds. Jose and Ratcliff (2004) found gender differences in depression, anxiety, and psychosomatic complaints in a sample of 10 - 20 year-olds. These differences were not consistent with the results of the present study.

There are three possible explanations for this difference between the findings of this study and past studies. Size of the sample of females, the age of the participants in the sample, as well as measurement differences may account for this contradiction.

The first possible explanation for the divergence from the literature is the relative number of females that were included in this study was small ($n = 65$). In fact, one particular cell, females with Average to Above Average Parent Relations coupled with At-Risk to Clinically Significant Self-Esteem, had a cell size of 6 ($n = 6$). Small cell sizes significantly affected the power to detect meaningful differences between males and females (power = .278). In other words, based on the power of .278, there is approximately 70% probability of failing to detect a genuine difference between males and females.

The fact that there were so few females in this sample is interesting in itself. This sample consisted of a total sample of all students that completed the BASC-2 in a public school system of approximately 10,000 students. As noted previously, students complete the BASC-2 if they have been identified as having an emotional and behavioral disorder or are suspected as having one. This suggests that over the last 3 years in a school district of 10,000 students, only 65 females have been identified with EBD or were evaluated for EBD. This is consistent with previous research states that females are under-represented in special education (Oswald, Best, Coutinho, & Nagle, 2003).

Another explanation may be that the age range of this study's sample differed from past studies. Kubik et al. (2003) sampled 12 - 13 year olds only. Jose and Ratcliff (2004) surveyed children and adolescents ranging in age from 10 - 20 years. Some studies, like that conducted by Crawford et al. (2001), suggest that gender differences in internalizing problems do not emerge until puberty. Because this study included children as young as 8 years old, gender differences may not have been detected.

The third explanation for this difference is the manner in which internalizing problems is defined. Internalizing problems on the BASC-2 includes a wide range of internalizing-type problems such as atypicality (tendency to behave in a manner considered odd or strange), locus of control, social stress, anxiety, depression, and sense of inadequacy. Previous studies have examined gender differences in single disorders such as depression, rather than as an inclusive category (Leadbeater et al., 1995; Kubik,

70

et al., 2003; Jose & Ratcliff, 2004). This indicates that there is a possibility that the Internalizing Problems scale on the BASC-2 evaluates additional problems in which no gender differences can be detected.

Research Question 3

The third research question asked whether the degree of internalizing problems is related to the level of self-esteem. The results indicated that the degree of internalizing problems vary according to the level of self-esteem reported by at-risk children and adolescents. Specifically, children and adolescents with low self-esteem reported a higher degree of internalizing problems than those with average or better self-esteem. Likewise, children and adolescents with average or better self-esteem reported a lower degree of internalizing problems.

These results support those reported in the existing literature. Marsh et al. (2004) studied the relationship between self-esteem and a variety mental health conditions that fall under the category of internalizing problems. Specifically, there was a moderate negative correlation between self-esteem and anxiety, depression, and somatic complaints. Erkolahti et al. (2003) studied the relationship between self-image and depressive symptoms. Strong negative correlations between self-image and depressive symptoms were noted.

There were differences between this study and the existing studies. Marsh et al. (2004) specifically studied Canadian middle school students, Reid (2004) studied college students, and Erkolahti et al. (2003) studied 8th grade Finnish students. Each of them measured self-esteem differently. None of them investigated internalizing problems as a single cluster of symptoms.

71

Despite these key differences, the results were consistent. The degree of internalizing problems reported by children and adolescents was related to the level of self-esteem. This implies that the present study expands on the existing literature by confirming the results using a sample with a wider age level, a broader ethnic composition, and measuring internalizing problems as a single cluster using different instrumentation.

These results suggest that children and adolescents with low levels of self-esteem may be more vulnerable to internalizing problems; those with high self-esteem may be protected from internalizing problems. This provides support for efforts to promote self-esteem in children and adolescents. Targeted efforts could be made in the school setting at early ages.

Research Question 4

The fourth research asked whether the combination of quality of relations with parents, gender, and level of self-esteem have a predictive relationship with the degree of internalizing problems reported by at-risk children and adolescents. Results indicated that each of these factors had a predictive relationship with internalizing problems; however, these factors taken together have a significantly stronger predictive relationship with internalizing problems. Specifically, being female appears to put an individual at a slight, but significant, risk for internalizing problems. However, this significance may be the result of the small number of females in the sample. Adding a poor quality of parent-child relationship strengthens this prediction. Finally, adding low self-esteem further strengthens the prediction of internalizing problems.

72

This study is the first of its kind to examine these factors together in one study. As such, it provides preliminary evidence that the combination of being female, having a poor parent-child relationship, and low self-esteem increases the risk of internalizing problems. Given the potential debilitating effects of internalizing problems, this study speaks to the importance of further investigation of these factors as they could guide practitioners to target certain groups for preventing or coping with internalizing problems.

Strengths

This study had noteworthy strengths. Strengths were evident with the sample, instrumentation, and design of the study. In addition, the findings resulting from this study significantly contribute to the existing literature on internalizing problems.

The first strength was with the sample collected for this study. Not only was it a large sample, it was assumed that the sample of students that completed the BASC-2 were roughly equivalent to the demographics of the school district studied. If that was indeed the case, then the sample collected for this study was a relatively diverse sample. These were benefits because much of the research reviewed used small and/or homogeneous samples.

Second, the BASC-2 has strong technical characteristics and up-to-date norms. In addition, all data was collected from the BASC-2, rather than from an array of various instruments. This is different than many of the previous studies, most of which used several instruments to collect data, and/or used instruments with outdated norms.

Third, the design of the study allowed for the examination of interactions between variables, as well as the investigation of predictive relationships between them. No other study to date has attempted to examine these particular variables using these design characteristics.

The final and perhaps most important strength of this study, was its contribution to the literature. The results not only confirmed and extended the results of past similar studies, it generated new knowledge in the area of internalizing problems. Specifically, the findings suggest that gender, the quality of parent relations, and level of self-esteem individually have a predictive relationship with internalizing problems. In addition, these variables taken together appear to strengthen the prediction of internalizing problems.

Limitations

Sample

As with any research project, this study had limitations. Limitations to be considered include issues with the sample, internal and external validity, and measurement. Each of these limitations, as well as their implications, will be discussed.

One significant limitation was the number of females that were a part of this sample. Although the total sample was large, the number of females in the study was small. As noted earlier, this affected the power of the statistical tests to detect gender differences in relationship to any of the variables. With a greater number of females in the sample, gender differences, as well as interactions would have been more valid.

Another limitation was the wide age range sampled. The initial intent was to focus on adolescents ages 12 - 18. However, to obtain an adequate sample size with the

74

available dataset, the age range needed to widen to include children ages 8 - 11. Combining these ages resulted in a sample that included pre-pubertal and pubertal adolescents. The findings of this study may have been different for either one of these groups taken alone as the focal study sample.

Finally, the data collected did not identify the race of the individuals within this sample. As with age, it is not known whether the findings of this study would have differed for individuals of varying races.

Internal Validity

Because this was a causal-comparative study, direct causality cannot be determined from these results. Although the findings of this study indicate that the quality of parent relations and the level of self-esteem are related to the level of internalizing problems, it does not mean that poor parent-child relationships or low self-esteem caused internalizing problems. It is possible that internalizing problems caused problems within the parent-child relationship and self-esteem or that these factors mutually influence each other. It is also possible that a confounding variable influenced the results. These limitations with regard to internal validity must be considered with any causal-comparative study.

External Validity

The external validity of this study must also be considered when interpreting the results. The sample used in this study consisted of children and adolescents that attend public school in northeastern Minnesota and either have an emotional and behavioral disorder, or were suspected of having one. As a result, these results may not generalize to children and adolescents with dissimilar characteristics.

Measurement

With regard to measurement, this study used self-reports. This was chosen because self-report is considered to be the best way to measure internalizing problems, because of their insidious nature (Reynolds & Kamphaus, 2004). However, coupling it with direct observation could have strengthened the self-report data. Thus, using solely self-report data may be viewed as a limitation.

Recommendations for Future Research

Future research will continue to deepen and broaden our current understanding of internalizing disorders as experienced by children and adolescents. Efforts may include exact replication of this study, replications with slight modifications to the design of this study, or using the framework of this study to include additional variables. Any of these efforts would significantly contribute to the literature on internalizing disorders in children and adolescents.

Researchers may wish to replicate this study with a larger sample of females. This would increase the statistical ability to more reliably detect gender differences in internalizing problems as well as parent relations, and self-esteem. Not only would a larger sample of females allow the detection of possible gender differences, interactions between these factors could more effectively be addressed. This alone would significantly expand on the current knowledge base in the field. Exact replication of this study with larger sample size would also allow for more specific analysis of the data. For example, researchers could examine whether children and adolescents with above average self-esteem or parent relations differ from those with average self-esteem or parent relations

76

in their internalizing symptoms. Likewise, differences in the level of internalizing problems experienced by those with at-risk self-esteem or and clinically significant self-esteem could be examined. Interactions between these narrowly defined factors could also be investigated. Examination of these slight distinctions could have significant implications for practitioners targeting preventative efforts.

Another potential direction for research would be to examine the role of gender, parent relations, and self-esteem with internalizing problems using different measurement tools. For example, the BASC-2 evaluates self-esteem as an overall global quality (Reynolds & Kamphaus, 2004). Other instruments that measure various types of self-esteem would further clarify the role that self-esteem plays with internalizing problems. Replication of this study with different measurement tools would clarify the relationships between these variables.

Longitudinal studies would also help clarify the relationships between variables. This study found that level of reported internalizing problems differed according to the quality of parent relationships. Likewise, the level of reported internalizing varied according to level of self-esteem. Longitudinal investigations would help clarify whether poor parent relationships and low self-esteem cause internalizing problems or if existing internalizing problems cause subsequent impairments in parent-child relationships and self-esteem.

Using multiple methods to measure these variables would enhance the credibility of this study's findings. For example, internalizing-type symptoms could be measured by self-report and verified through observations. Parent-child relationships could be measured by child as well as parent reports. Triangulation of data collection method lends credibility to the data collected (Patton, 2002).

Future research may also include additional variables to further clarify the relationships between parent relations, gender, self-esteem, and internalizing problems. Adding variables such as age and race would determine whether the relationships between these variables differ according to the age and the race of the individual. This too would have significant implications for those who work with children and adolescents.

Summary and Conclusion

Internalizing disorders are prevalent among children and adolescents. The effects of these problems are often debilitating. Given this, it is important for researchers to continue attempts to advance the understanding of these disorders. Continued progress in this area should focus on identifying additional factors or combination of factors related to internalizing disorders as well as the effectiveness of prevention and intervention programs. Doing so may reduce the likelihood of internalizing problems emerging or may reduce the negative affects that are often associated with these problems.

REFERENCES

Achenbach, T. M. (1966). The classification of children's psychiatric symptoms: A factor analytic study. *Psychological Monographs, 80, (No. 615).*

Achenbach, T. M. (1985). Assessment and taxonomy of child and adolescent psychopathology. Beverly Hills, CA: Sage Publications.

Achenbach, T. M. (1991). *Manual for the Youth Self-Report and 1991 Profile.* Burlington: University of Vermont, Department of Psychiatry.

Achenbach, T. M. (2006). Achenbach System of Empirically Based Assessment. Retrieved on October 6, 2006 from, http://www.aseba.org/

Achenbach, T. M. & Edelbrock, C. (1978). The classification of child psychopathology: A review and analysis of empirical efforts. *Psychological Bulletin, 85,* 1275-1301.

Achenbach, T. M. & McConaughy, S. H. (1996). Relations between DSM-IV and empirically based assessment. *School Psychology Review, 25*(3), 329-342.

American Guidance Services Inc. (2005). BASC-2 ASSIST Plus[TM] Scoring and Reporting System (Version 1.0) [Computer software]. Circle Pines, MN: Author.

Andersson, L. (1981). *The Psychosomatic Symptoms Scale.* Stockholm Gerontology Research Center, Stockholm.

Asher, S. R., Hymel, S., & Renshaw, P. D. (1984). Loneliness in children. *Child Development, 55,* 1456-1464.

Beck, A. T., Ward, C., Mendelson, M., Mock, J., Erbaugh, J. (1961). An inventory for depression. *Archives in General Psychiatry, 4,* 561-571.

Birleson, P. (1981). The validity of depressive disorder in childhood and the development of a self-rating scale: A research report. *Journal of Child Psychology and Psychiatry, 22,* 73-88.

Birmaher, B., Ryan, N. D. Williamson, D. E., Brent, D. A., Kaufman, J., Dahl, R. E., et al. (1996). Childhood and adolescent depression: A review of the past 10 years. Part I. *Journal of the American Academy of Child & Adolescent Psychiatry, 35,* 1427-1439.

Blythe, D., Hill, J., Theil, K. (1982). Early adolescents' significant others: Grade and gender differences in perceived relationships with familial and nonfamilial adults and young people. *Journal of Youth and Adolescence, 11,* 425-450.

Bradburn, N. M. (1969). *The structure of psychological well-being.* Chicago: Aldine.

Breakwell, G. & Rose, D. (2000). Research: Theory and method. In G. M. Breakwell, S., Hammond, & C. Fife-Schaw (Eds.), *Research methods in psychology* (2nd ed., pp. 5-21). Thousand Oaks, CA: Sage.

Byrne, B. (2000). Relationships between anxiety, fear, self-esteem, and coping strategies in adolescence. *Adolescence, 35*(137), 201-215.

Compton, S. N., Burns, B. J., Egger, H. L., & Robertson, E. (2002). Review of the evidence base for treatment of childhood psychopathology: Internalizing disorders. *Journal of Consulting and Clinical Psychology, 70*(6), 1240-1266.

Costello, A. J., Edelbrock, C. S. Dulcan, M. K. Kalas, R., & Klaric, S. H. (1984). *Testing of the NIMH Diagnostic Interview Schedule for Children (DISC) in a clinical population. Final report to the Center for Epidemiological Studies, National Institute of Mental Health.* Pittsburgh: University of Pittsburgh.

Crawford, Cohen, Midlarsky, & Brook (2001). Internalizing symptoms in adolescents: Gender differences in vulnerability to parental distress and discord. *Journal of Research on Adolescence, 11*(1), 95-118.

Delaney, M. E. (1996). Across the transition to adolescence: Qualities of parent/adolescent relationships and adjustment. *Journal of Early Adolescence, 16*(3), 274-300.

Derogatis, R. C., Lipman, R. S., Rickles, K., Uhlenhuth, E. H.. & Covi, L. (1974). The Hopkins Symptoms Checklist (HSCL). *Behavioral Science, 19,* 1-15.

Erkolahti, R. Ilonen, T. Saarijarvi, S., & Terho, P. (2003). Self-image and depressive symptoms among adolescents in a non-clinical sample. *Nord Journal of Psychiatry, 57,* 447-451.

Faul, F. & Erdfelder, E. (1992). G*Power: A priori, post-hoc, and compromise power analyses for MS-DOS [Computer software]. Bonn, FRG: Bonn University, Department of Psychology.

Field, A. (2005). *Discovering statistics using SPSS* (2nd ed). Thousand Oaks, CA: Sage.

Fife-Schaw, C. (2000). Levels of measurement. In G. M. Breakwell, S. Hammond, & C. Fife-Schaw (Eds.), *Research methods in psychology* (2nd ed., pp. 147-157). Thousand Oaks, CA: Sage.

Garber, J. (2000). Development and depression. In A. J. Sameroff, M. Lewis, & S. M. Miller (Eds.), *Handbook of developmental psychopathology* (2nd ed., pp. 467-490. New York: Plenum Press.

Gerris, J. R., Houtmans, M. J. M., Kwaaitaal-Roosen, E. M. G., Schipper, J.C., Vermulst, A. A., & Janssens, J. M. A. M. (1998). *Parents, Adolescents and Young Adults in Dutch Families: A longitudinal study.* Nijmegen: Institute of Family Studies, University of Nijmegen.

Hammond, S. (2000). Using psychometric tests. In G. M. Breakwell, S. Hammond, & C. Fife-Schaw (Eds.), *Research methods in psychology* (2nd ed., pp. 147-157). Thousand Oaks, CA: Sage.

Howell, D. C. (2004). *Fundamental statistics for the behavioral sciences* (5th ed.). Belmont, CA: Brooks/Cole.

Jose, P. E. & Ratcliff, V. (2004). Stressor frequency and perceived intensity as predictors of internalizing symptoms: Gender and age differences in adolescence. *New Zealand Journal of Psychology, 33*(3), 145-154.

Kliewer, W., Murrelle, L., & Meja, R. (2001). Exposure to violence against a family member and internalizing symptoms in Columbian adolescents: The protective effects of family support. *Journal of Community and Clinical Psychology, 69*(6), 971-982.

Kling, K. C., Hyde, J. S., Showers, C. J., & Buswell, B. N. (1999). Gender differences in self-esteem: A meta-analysis. *Psychological Bulletin, 125*(4), 470-500.

Kovacs, M. (1981). Rating scale to assess depression in school-age children. *Acta Paedepsychiatry, 46,* 305-310.

Kovacs, M. (1985). The Children's Depression Inventory (CDI). *Psychopharmacology Bulletin, 21,* 995-998.

Kubik, M. Y., Lytle, L. A., Birnbaum, A. S., Murray, D. M., & Perry, C. L. (2003). Prevalence and correlates of depressive symptoms in young adolescents. *American Journal of Health Behavior, 27*(5), 546-553.

La Greca, A. M. (1999). *Social anxiety scales for children and adolescents.* Miami, FL: Author.

Laurent, J. & Landau, S. (1993). Conditional probabilities in the diagnosis of depressive and anxiety disorders. *School Psychology Review, 22*(1). Retrieved March 3, 2005, from MasterFILE Premier database.

Leedy, P.D., & Ormrod, J.E. (2005). *Practical research: Planning and design* (8th Ed.). Upper Saddle River, NJ: Prentice-Hall.

Leadbeater, B. J., Blatt, S. J. & Quinlan, D. M. (1995). Gender-linked vulnerabilities to depressive symptoms, stress, and problem behaviors in adolescents. *Journal of Research on Adolescence, 5*(1), 1-29.

Lewinsohn, P. M. & Essau, C. A. (2002). Depression in adolescents. In I. Gotlib & C. Hammen (Eds.), *Handbook of depression* (pp. 541-559). New York: Guilford Press.

Lillehoj, C. J., Trudeau, L., Spoth, R., & Wickrama, K. A. (2004). Internalizing, social competence, and substance initiation: Influence of gender moderation and a preventative intervention. *Substance Use and Misuse, 39*(6), 963-991.

Loeber, R., Stouthamer-Loeber, M., & White, H. R. (1999). Developmental aspects of delinquency and internalizing problems and their association with persistent juvenile substance use between ages 7 and 18. *Journal of Clinical Child Psychology, 28*(3), 322-332.

Manders, W. A., Scholte, R. H., Janssens, J. A., & De Bruyn, E. E. (2006). Adolescent personality, problem behaviour and the quality of the parent-adolescent relationship. *European Journal of Personality, 20,* 237-254.

Margolin, S. (2006). African American youths with internalizing difficulties: Relation to social support and activity involvement. *Children & Schools, 28*(3), 135-144.

Marsh, H. W. (1992). *Self-Description Questionnaire II: Manual.* Sydney, Australia: University of Western Sydney, SELF Research Centre.

Marsh, H. W., Parada, R. H., & Ayotte, V. (2004). A multidimensional perspective of relations between self-concept (Self-Description Questionnaire II) and adolescent mental health (Youth Self-Report). *Psychological Assessment, 16*(1), 27-41.

McConaughy, S., & Skiba, R. (1993). Comorbidity of externalizing and internalizing problems. *School Psychology Review, 22*(3), 421. Retrieved October 23, 2006 from the MasterFILE Premier database.

Menard, S. (1995). *Applied logistic regression analysis.* Sage university paper series on quantitative applications in the social sciences, 7-106. Thousand Oaks, CA: Sage.

Minnesota Department of Education (2005). Student Demographics. Retrieved December 30, 2006, from http://education.state.mn.us/ReportCard2005/schoolDistrictInfo.do?SCHOOL_NUM=000&DISTRICT_NUM=0709&DISTRICT_TYPE=01

National Association of School Psychologists (2002). Position statement on students with emotional and behavioral disorders. Retrieved March 3, 2005, from www.nasponline.org

National Association of School Psychologists (2003). Position statement on mental health services in the schools. Retrieved February 28, 2005, from www.nasponline.org

National Commission for the Protection of Human Subjects of Biomedical and Behavioral Research (1979). The Belmont report: Ethical principles and guidelines for the protection of human subjects of research. Retrieved March 12, 2006, from http://www.nihtraining.com/ohsrsite/guidelines/belmont.html

Nunnally, J. C. (1978). *Psychometric theory*. New York: McGraw-Hill.

Offer, D., Ostrov, E., Howard, K. I., & Dolan, S. (1989). *The Offer Self-Image Questionnaire for Adolescents: A manual, 4th ed.* Chicago: Center for the Study of Adolescence.

Oswald, D. P., Best, A. M., Coutinho, M. J., & Nagle, H. A. (2003). Trends in special education identification rates of boys and girls: A call for research and change. *Exceptionality, 11*(4), 223-237.

Patton, M. (2002). *Qualitative research and evaluation methods*. Thousand Oaks, CA: Sage.

Pine, D. S., Cohen, E., Cohen, P., & Brook, J. (1999). Adolescent depressive symptoms as predictors of adult depression. Moodiness or mood disorder? *American Journal of Psychiatry, 156,* 133-135.

Quatman, T. & Watson, C. M. (2001). Gender differences in self-esteem: An exploration of domains. The Journal of Genetic Psychology, 162, 93-117.

Radloff, L. S. (1977). The CES-D scale: A self-report depression scale for research in the general population. *Applied Psychological Measures, 1,* 385-401.

Rapport, M. D., Denney, C. B., Chung, K., & Hustace, K. (2001). Internalizing behavior problems and scholastic achievement in children: Cognitive and behavioral pathways as mediators of outcome. *Journal of Clinical Child Psychology, 30*(4), 536-551.

Reid, A. (2004). Gender and sources of subjective well-being. *Sex Roles, 51*(11&12), 617-629.

Reid, M., Landesman, S., Treder, R., & Jaccard, J. (1989). "My family and friends:" Six to twelve year-old children's perception's of social support. *Child Development, 60,* 896-910.

Reynolds, C. R. & Kamphaus, R. W. (2004). *Behavior Assessment System for Children Manual* (2nd ed.). Circle Pines, MN: American Guidance Services, Inc.

Reynolds, C. R. & Richmond, B. O. (1979). What I think and feel. A revised measure of children's manifest anxiety. *Journal of Abnormal Child Psychology, 25,* 15-20.

Reynolds, W. M. (1990). Introduction to the nature and study of internalizing disorders in children and adolescents. *School Psychology Review, 19*(2), 137-142.

Reynolds, W. M. (Ed.). (1992). *Internalizing disorders in children and adolescents* (Vol. 1). New York: John Wiley & Sons.

Ronnlund, M. & Karlsson, E. (2006). The relation between dimensions of attachment and internalizing or externalizing problems during adolescence. *The Journal of Genetic Psychology, 167*(1). 47-63.

Rosenberg, M. (1965). *Society and the adolescent self-image.* Princeton University Press.

Scholte, R. H., van Lieshout, C. F. & van Aken, M. A. G. (2001). Perceived relational support in adolescence: Traits, configurations, and adolescent adjustment. *Journal of Research on Adolescence, 11,* 71-94.

Schweitzer, R. D., Seth-Smith, M., & Callan, V. (1992). The relationship between self-esteem and psychological adjustment in young adolescents. *Journal of Adolescence, 15,* 83-97.

Spielberger, C. D., Gorsuch, R. L., Lushene, R. E., Vagg, P. R., & Jacobs, G. A. (1983). *Manual for the State-Trait Anxiety Inventory.* Palo Alto, CA: Consulting Psychologists Press.

SPSS Inc. (2004). SPSS[TM] for Windows (Version 13.0) [Computer software]. Chicago, IL: Author.

Steinberg, L., & Silverberg, S. B. (1986). The vicissitudes of autonomy in early adolescence. *Child Development, 57,* 841-851.

U. S. Surgeon General (1999). Mental health: A report of the Surgeon General. Retrieved February 1, 2006, from http://www.surgeongeneral.gov/library/mentalhealth/home.html

Wang, M. Q., Fitzhugh, E. C. & Westerfield, R. C. (1994). Predicting smoking status by symptoms of depression for US adolescents. *Psychological Reports, 75,* 911-914.

Wu, P., Hoven, C., Bird, H., Moore, R., Cohen, P., Algeria, M., Dulcan, M., Goodman, S., McCue Horwitz., S., Lichtman, J., Narrow, W., Rae., D., Reigier, D., & Roper, M. (1999). Depressive and disruptive disorders and mental health utilization in children and adolescents. *Journal of the American Academy of Child and Adolescent Psychiatry, 38*(9), 1081-1092.

www.ingramcontent.com/pod-product-compliance
Lightning Source LLC
Chambersburg PA
CBHW081159270326
41930CB00014B/3214